ALONG THE RAILS

A Survey of Maine's Historic Railroad Buildings

KIRK F. MOHNEY, EDITOR

Maine Preservation
Portland, Maine
2000

Maine Preservation

Designed by Mahan Graphics, Bath, Maine

Printed by J.S. McCarthy, Augusta, Maine

All rights reserved

Copyright © 2000

ISBN 0-935447-15-6

Front Cover:

Maine Central Railroad Station, Warren, c. 1910

Photos and drawings courtesy of the Maine Historic Preservation Commission, except *Bath*, page 60, courtesy of Maine Maritime Museum.

Back Cover:

Elevation drawing of Passenger Station [Maine Central Railroad] for West Waterville, c. 1870

Foreword 5

Preface 7

Introduction & Acknowledgments 9

Chapter I ~ railway development in maine
   Carlton J. Corliss 15

Chapter II ~ railroad passenger stations in maine:
         an overview of their architectural
         development
   Roger G. Reed 37

Chapter III ~ a catalogue of railroad stations
   Sylvanus Doughty and Kirk F. Mohney 57

Chapter IV ~ a catalogue of railroad buildings
   Sylvanus Doughty and Kirk F. Mohney 101

Bibliography 115

Appendix A
   Sylvanus Doughty and Kirk F. Mohney 121

Appendix B
   Earle G. Shettleworth, Jr. and Roger G. Reed 143

"Waiting for the First Ride," Maine Central Railroad Station, Harmony, August 19, 1912

FOREWORD

Maine's historic railroad buildings are not only a link to your past, but are becoming an important element of your transportation future. Growing concern over automobile congestion, environmental and social impacts, and fiscal sustainability requires a look beyond highway expansion to meet Maine's mobility needs. Passenger rail service is now viewed as an essential element of an integrated, multimodal transportation system. Passenger rail can support the revitalization of our service centers and serve as a much needed antidote for sprawl.

The foundation stones are now being laid for the rebirth of passenger rail in Maine. With the arrival of AMTRAK service from Boston to Portland to Brunswick, we have a beginning. Rehabilitation of rail from Brunswick to Rockland was secured by Maine voters in 1999 as was the beginning of rehabilitation on the Calais Branch.

Some stations are to be new while others fortunately involve the restoration of former stations. In the case of Brunswick, a new station is planned at the site of the former station. Planning is also under way for a new kind of station that serves to interconnect rail, motorcoach, air, and marine passenger services.

Those who seek to re-establish passenger rail will find this book instructive. It offers a chance to become reacquainted with site and design considerations. Hopefully, it will spur efforts to preserve these structures and, in special circumstances, allow for reuse as part of Maine's rail future.

The Maine Department of Transportation appreciates having the occasion to, once again, collaborate with the Maine Historic Preservation Commission on a project of common interest.

JOHN G. MELROSE, COMMISSIONER
Maine Department of Transportation

The FLYING YANKEE,
Old Orchard Beach, c. 1940

PREFACE

Fifty years ago rail travel was still king in Maine. Like many of my generation, trains captured my youthful imagination. My favorite Sunday drive with my parents was along Commercial Street in Portland to watch the engines, freight cars, and tank cars slowly move down the center of that broad waterfront thoroughfare. When I was four, I was treated to my first train ride, a Sunday afternoon trip with my mother and sister from Union Station to Old Orchard Beach, where we were met by my father, who had covered the same distance by car on Route 1 in order to provide our return transportation.

As I entered my teens, passenger service in Maine ended, thus closing the broad network of stations which had bound so many lives together. At the age of thirteen, I witnessed the proud tower of Union Station crash to the ground as an elegant granite building, which had meant so much to so many, was reduced to rubble. Soon another proud tower fell in Bangor, joined by the destruction of dozens of more modest frame stations and support buildings across the state.

Nearly four decades later, as the hope of passenger rail service in Maine dawns again, the Maine Historic Preservation Commission, with the generous support of an ISTEA grant from the Maine Department of Transportation, has undertaken to locate the state's remaining train stations and related structures. To our surprise, our initial estimate of two hundred structures was revised to three hundred as survey work progressed. Railroad stations have proved to be particularly adaptable, from a residence in West Minot to a car dealership in South Paris and an airport in Princeton. These surviving structures are presented in the context of the history of rail service and railroad stations in Maine. This is a book for those Mainers of all ages for whom the romance of the rails is still very much alive.

EARLE G. SHETTLEWORTH, JR., DIRECTOR
Maine Historic Preservation Commission

View of the Maine Central Railroad yard at Vanceboro, c. 1890

INTRODUCTION

In an article titled "Beyond the Information Revolution" (*Atlantic Monthly*, October, 1999), the social scientist Peter F. Drucker makes the observation that the railroad was the first truly revolutionary outcome of the Industrial Revolution. Unlike the development of the steam engine which preceded it, the railroad fundamentally altered human society and economies with its ability to link people and goods in ways and at speeds that had hitherto been unthinkable. From our perspective at the dawn of the twenty-first century, decades after local passenger rail service ceased in Maine and at a time when numerous branch lines have been abandoned altogether, it is difficult to fully appreciate the historic importance of railroads and the impact they had on the communities through which they passed. Although a renaissance of sorts appears to be in the making for limited passenger rail service in Maine, it is highly unlikely that we will ever witness again the network of railroads that were a vital part of life in the late nineteenth and early twentieth centuries.

The history of railroad development in Maine is largely the story of the local promotion of rail lines whose routes and connections were chosen to advance local economic interests. The intensity and extent of these efforts underscores the perceived value of a railroad connection and the expanded economic opportunities that would result. Since 1832, when the Maine Legislature issued its first three charters, scores of railroad companies have been incorporated in the state. Many of these proposed railroads were never more than the ambitious ideas of their incorporators. However, a large number were eventually built in one form or another, although it often took many years to raise the necessary capital for construction. With the possible exception of the Bangor & Aroostook Railroad, these railroads were not conceived on a grand plan of main lines fed by a network of trunk lines. More often than not, they were developed with narrowly focused goals, such as providing a means to access specific resources or to link particular destinations. For example, the state's two earliest railroads were built to transport lumber from harvesting areas to sawmill complexes, whereas the development of a rail connection with Quebec energized the efforts of railroad promoters in Belfast, Portland, and Wiscasset. Eventually, most of these individual lines — with the notable exception of the narrow gauge railroads — were incorporated into one of five principal rail systems through long term lease agreements or outright purchase. An overview of Maine's

Portland & Rumford Falls Railway Engine No. 3 alongside the station in Livermore, c. 1910

railroad history, which was written in 1953 by Carlton J. Corliss, is the subject of Chapter I. A list of the railroad charters granted by the Legislature prior to World War II, and the subsequent history of those charters is found in Appendix A.

The tangible remnants of Maine's railroad history are still in evidence — if you look. In addition to active rail lines and facilities, several hundred railroad related buildings and structures are still in existence, as are numerous abandoned rail corridors, many of which are being used today for recreational purposes. Railroad history is being preserved through the efforts of train clubs, historical societies, museums, and private citizens who own and care for everything from documentary records and buildings to operational rolling stock. It has also been the subject of numerous books and articles. On the other hand, a great deal has been lost since the end of World War II. Foremost among the buildings that no longer stand are numerous railroad stations, including the four largest and most architecturally significant examples that were ever erected in Maine. Functional obsolescence has led to the wide scale demolition of certain types of railroad structures, and many others are deteriorating from a lack of basic maintenance. Railroad buildings are often easily moved, and many have been relocated from their original sites. Although this practice has resulted in the preservation of endangered buildings, it severs a community's connection to its railroad history — particularly if a building is moved out of town — and fundamentally alters their historic context.

In the late 1980s, the Maine Historic Preservation Commission began an informal survey to identify the extant railroad stations in the state. At that time it was evident that a comprehensive survey of all surviving railroad related buildings was needed to document these endangered historic properties. This project became a reality in 1994 when the Commission was awarded a grant from the Maine Department of Transportation. The survey was funded through the Enhancement program of the Intermodal Surface Transportation Efficiency Act of 1991 (ISTEA), a new component of Federal transportation funding which gave state transportation departments the opportunity to fund non-traditional transportation projects.

Fieldwork conducted in 1995-96 by architect and MRG, Inc./DownEast Rail president Sylvanus Doughty resulted in the identification of more than 300 railroad related buildings, a large percentage of which still stand adjacent to historic railroad rights-of-way. In addition to passenger stations, the survey recorded a wide range of other building types, including freight houses, engine houses, tool houses, and a handful of extant water tanks. Conversations with knowledgeable local residents helped to locate a number of buildings that had been moved and converted to other uses such as single family dwellings. Although a project of this scope and short duration will overlook some examples, every effort was made to create a complete picture of the resource.

In Chapter II, architectural historian and former MHPC staff member Roger G. Reed analyzes the design of railroad stations in Maine. Information pertaining to existing railroad stations and other railroad related buildings is presented in Chapters III and IV, respectively. Finally, Appendix B contains an inventory of historic railroad building drawings that are located in the collections of the MHPC and the Maine Historical Society.

View of the Canadian Pacific Railroad Station, Somerset Jct., c. 1910

In its grant application to the MDOT, the Commission pointed out that many historic railroad related buildings continue to occupy their original sites along both active and inactive railroad corridors, and that the resumption of rail service or the reuse of such corridors for alternative modes of transportation might offer opportunities to reuse these buildings. The MDOT's long term planning goals include a passenger rail component that is designed to both reduce highway congestion and to broaden tourism opportunities. Since 1987 it has acquired several rail corridors in order to preserve the option of restoring rail service on them, or for use as recreational trails. The Department has also obtained a number of historic railroad buildings, including the former Maine Central Railroad station, engine house and turntable in Rockland. Former stations that stand along these lines may be in a position to be reused in a rejuvenated passenger rail system. Where the possibility of restored rail service is remote, other uses for these buildings in non-traditional and multi-modal transportation systems should be explored. For example, to what use might historic railroad related buildings be put along those portions of Maine's large network of recreational trails that follow abandoned rail corridors? Furthermore, how might the Enhancement provisions of TEA-21 (the successor transportation bill to ISTEA) be used to promote the preservation of these buildings? These questions and others like them need to become part of the debate about the use and development of a broadly defined transportation system in twenty-first century Maine.

On behalf of the Maine Historic Preservation Commission, I wish to take this opportunity to thank the Maine Department of Transportation for its financial support in both the survey and publication phases of this project. The Department's commitment to this project is an acknowledgment that railroads and historic railroad related buildings can and will be part of the state's multi-modal transportation network. In our quest to identify historic railroad related buildings we relied on the input of municipal officials and local historical societies, and their interest is deeply appreciated. The cooperation of individual property owners was essential to the success of the survey. They not only granted permission to photograph their buildings, but often provided important historical information about them. Among the railroad companies, the Bangor & Aroostook was especially helpful in granting access to its facilities. I am grateful to the staffs of the Maine State Archives and the Maine State Library for their assistance in locating documents and other materials pertaining to Maine's railroad history. Finally, I would like to acknowledge the assistance of Emmons Lancaster, who shared information about a number of Maine Central buildings and facilities; Richard T. Howard, who provided a number of station views; as well as Doug Hutchinson and Robert T. Lord from whose books on Maine railroads several historic images of extant depots were obtained.

KIRK F. MOHNEY

**Locomotive PIONEER,
c. 1865**

CHAPTER I

Railway Development in Maine
Carlton J. Corliss

PIONEER RAILROADS

Maine's railway development began in 1832, when Andrew Jackson was President of the United States and when there were only 200 miles of railroad and a few locomotives in North America. In January of that year the seat of our State government was moved from Portland to Augusta, and it was during the first session of the Legislature, meeting in the new State House, that Maine's first two railway charters were granted to the Old Town Railroad and the Calais Railway Company.

Under the Old Town charter, Maine's first railroad was built for the purpose of transporting lumber. It extended from Bangor to Old Town, a distance of 11 miles. As might be expected, it was a crude affair, constructed of 6"x 6" wooden rails, capped with thin, narrow strips of iron, each 12 feet in length, to provide a running surface for the wheels.

The first locomotive to turn a wheel in Maine ran over this railroad on November 6, 1836. The engine was built by the Stephensons in England and brought across the Atlantic on the deck of a sailing vessel. Appropriately named the "Pioneer," Maine's first locomotive weighed only a few tons. Its wheels were of wood with iron hubs and tires. It had no cab, no headlight, no whistle, no cowcatcher, and of course, it burned wood for fuel. Teams of horses were employed to do the switching of cars and to substitute for the locomotive when a breakdown occurred.

For many years this pioneer railroad, known widely as "General Veazie's Railroad," was controlled and operated by General Samuel Veazie, the Lumber King of the Penobscot and the owner of more than fifty sawmills in the Bangor-Old Town area.

The Calais Railway Company built a two mile wooden railroad between Calais and Milltown in the late 1830s to serve the lumber industry. It was operated by horse power until 1852, when it became the Calais and Baring Railway Company and began operating a steam locomotive.[1]

Locomotive LION with owner Cornelius Sullivan standing on the right, 1897

Another pioneer logging road, built of wooden rails capped with strap iron, was the Franklin Railroad, an 8-mile line between Whitneyville and Machiasport in Washington County. It was opened in 1843. One of its early locomotives — the "Lion" — is on display at the Maine State Museum. At the north end of Moosehead Lake there was, as early as 1847, a wooden railroad, 3 miles in length, used to convey lumbermen and lumbermen's supplies from the lake to the headwaters of the Penobscot River. The Moosehead Lake Railway — a primitive affair if ever there was one — was operated by ox-power. Holman F. Day featured it in one of his novels; another writer referred to its "cud-chewing, tail-switching locomotive" as a "Bullgine." The gauge of this railroad was 3 feet 6 inches, and it probably was the first narrow-gauge railroad in the United States.

Boston & Maine Railroad

While short lumber roads were springing up in Northern and Eastern Maine, important developments were taking place elsewhere. Boston, with 75,000 inhabitants at the time its first railroad was opened in 1835,

CHAPTER I

Locomotives LION (left) and TIGER (right), 1897, before being shipped to Portland

was growing rapidly under the impetus of railway development and was soon to hold the distinction of being the nation's largest railway center, with lines fanning out like spokes from the hub of a wheel. Two of these lines were destined to figure prominently in Maine railway history: The Boston & Maine Railroad which ran from Boston to Portland by way of Haverhill and Dover, also known as the "Interior Line;" and the Eastern Railroad which ran from Boston to Portland by way of Newburyport and Portsmouth, also known as the "Shore Line." Both of these lines are now included in the Boston & Maine System, but for many years they were very strong competitors.

The "Shore Line" — which was known in Maine as the Portland, Saco & Portsmouth Railroad — brought its rails up to Portland on November 1, 1842, giving that city its first railway service and its first rail connection with Boston. Portland was then a city of about 20,000 people.

The Boston & Maine reached South Berwick, Maine, in 1843. Thereafter until 1873, through an agreement, it used the P. S. & P. tracks between that point and Portland. In 1873 the Boston & Maine

RAILWAY DEVELOPMENT IN MAINE

View of a work train on the Knox & Lincoln Railroad at a tidal cove of the Sheepscot River, Edgecomb — Newcastle town line, 1870s

extended its line to Portland, thus giving it complete independence of the Eastern Railroad. In the intervening years prior to 1884, when the Eastern was leased by the Boston & Maine, the two routes conducted a spirited contest for passengers and freight.

GRAND TRUNK RAILROAD

In the 1840s, Michigan, Indiana and Illinois were on the Western frontier, and they were attracting great numbers of homeseekers. An ever increasing export trade with Europe was being carried on in that region by way of the Erie Canal and the St. Lawrence River during the season of open navigation. For several months of each year, however, when the St. Lawrence was icebound, Montreal and Quebec were stranded and their business was virtually at a standstill. These cities keenly felt the need of rail connections with a year-round ice-free seaport and also with the rapidly expanding railway network in the Great Lakes region. Boston, Portland, Wiscasset, and Belfast were strong contenders for the proposed seaport railroad.

Portland was fortunate in having as a champion in the contest young, energetic and forceful John Alfred Poor, a lumberman's lawyer from Bangor. Poor was noted for getting things done. Through his efforts, the Atlantic & St. Lawrence Railroad Company was formed for the purpose of building a line from Montreal to Portland.

To gain support for the enterprise, Poor conducted an extraordinary campaign. He organized railroad conventions and mass meetings, addressed legislative bodies, groups of business leaders, farmers, and lumbermen in order to set forth the advantages of such a railroad. No crusader or evangelist was ever fired with greater zeal. He left no stone unturned in his efforts to get the railroad started. Finally, when the fight seemed to be almost won, word came that, through great pressure from business leaders in Boston, the Montreal Board of Trade was about to sign up with Boston instead of Portland.

Speaking of "rugged deeds and rugged men!" There are few incidents in American railroad history more exciting or more thrilling than the dash of John Alfred Poor by a succession of sleighs and sleds from Portland to Montreal in the dead of winter, in the teeth of a severe blizzard, in a desperate effort to reach there in time to plead the cause of Portland before it was too late. Immediately on his arrival at Montreal — without waiting to rest after his strenuous journey — Poor went before the Board leaders and eloquently presented the case of Portland versus Boston. He succeed in saving the situation, and Portland was finally chosen as the ocean terminal for the Montreal road. Out of this came the present Grand Trunk Railroad, completed in 1853, a railroad that contributed greatly to Portland's growth and importance as a seaport.

Maine Central Railroad

In 1845, the same year that the Montreal road received its charter, the Androscoggin & Kennebec Railroad was chartered to build a line from Danville Junction on the Atlantic & St. Lawrence (Grand Trunk) to Waterville, and the Penobscot & Kennebec Railroad was chartered to extend the Androscoggin & Kennebec line to Bangor. The former line

Maine Central Railroad's locomotive HALLOWELL, posed alongside the Worumbo Mill, Lisbon Falls, c. 1870

was completed to Waterville in 1849, and the first train entered Bangor over the latter road in August, 1855. These railroads, forming a continuous line between Danville Junction and Bangor, were consolidated in 1862 to form the Maine Central Railroad Company.

The present Maine Central Railroad through Brunswick and Augusta was originally a separate company known as the Kennebec & Portland, chartered in 1846 and completed in 1852. Its first president was former United States Senator George Evans of Gardiner, one of Maine's most distinguished sons. The line from Augusta to Waterville and on to Skowhegan was originally the Somerset & Kennebec Railroad, promoted by Abner Coburn, the bachelor governor of Maine, who after the consolidation became the first president of the Maine Central Railroad.

One cannot study the history of Maine railroads without being impressed by the great extent to which they were home enterprises, promoted by local people, built with funds raised within the State, and led by Maine men. This is something which cannot be said of railroads in many other parts of the country. For instance, in 1871, nine of the ten directors of the Maine Central were Maine men, and every director of the Androscoggin Railroad, the Knox & Lincoln Railroad, and the Bangor & Piscataquis Railroad resided in this state.

CHAPTER I

Battle of the Gauges

When Maine's first railroads were built there was no uniformity of gauge in this country. In 1871 there were more than 20 different gauges ranging all the way from 3 feet to 6 feet. One English manufacturer, George Stephenson, built some of his engines with a gauge of 4 feet, 8 inches, and since several of his engines were purchased and brought to the United States — for use in New England, New Jersey and Pennsylvania — some of the railway tracks were built to fit the locomotives. Because of the English influence, all railroads out of Boston, including the Boston & Maine Railroad leading up through Portsmouth and Kittery to Portland, had a gauge of 4 feet 8 inches, commonly referred to in early days as the "Boston Gauge" or "Narrow Gauge," and now known as the "Standard Gauge." The Kennebec & Portland and its extension through Brunswick and Augusta to Waterville and Skowhegan were also built on the "Boston Gauge."

However, the Grand Trunk was built with a gauge of 5 feet 6 inches between rails, known as the broad-gauge, sometimes called "John Poor's gauge," because John Poor was its leading advocate. Poor had a good reason for wanting a broad gauge. He was interested in building up the port of Portland. Boston had the advantage of excellent harbor and port facilities and more frequent sailings. Its business leaders wielded far more influence than did those of the much smaller city of Portland. To prevent Montreal traffic from being diverted to Boston, Poor had the Portland–Montreal line built with a broad gauge. The Grand Trunk set the style, and of course the Androscoggin & Kennebec, which had to use the tracks of the Grand Trunk to reach Portland, had to be built on the same broad gauge. Its eastern extension, the Penobscot & Kennebec, was also broad gauge. For the same reason, branch lines extending to Farmington and Solon were broad gauge.

This dual system of gauge created no end of problems. Whenever there was a break of gauge, as in Portland, Waterville and Kendall's Mills (now Fairfield), travelers had to change cars, sometimes depots, and all freight had to be transferred from the cars of one railroad to the cars of another. The Gauge question became an important political issue. The state was divided between "Broad Gauge Men" and "Narrow Gauge Men," and between "Broad Gauge Towns" and "Narrow Gauge Towns" (narrow gauge, in this instance meaning, 4 feet 8 inches).

RAILWAY DEVELOPMENT IN MAINE

THE BEST IS GOOD ENOUGH.

The Health, Pleasure Seeker's, Angler's, and Hunter's Line:

THE ❊ MAINE ❊ CENTRAL ❊ RAILROAD.

Fitted with every luxury of travel; run Palace Cars several times a day to and from Portland and the Charming Inland Retreats of Maine,

Poland Spring, Lake Auburn, Auburn, Lewiston, Maranacook, Oakland, Skowhegan, Newport, Dexter, Dover, Foxcroft, Monson, Greenville Junction

——— AND ———

KINEO: MOOSEHEAD LAKE,

The objective point in the early Spring of the Angler, in the Summer of the fashionable Tourist, and in the Fall of the Hunter, can now be reached several hours earlier than ever before from Boston and New York, and save fifty miles' travel by taking this line via Newport, Dexter, and Foxcroft; and it is the direct route to NICATOUS LAKE, WINN, DOBSIS and DUCK LAKES. It is also the Scenic Route to the famous resorts upon MT. DESERT, the adjacent coast of Maine, and the WHITE MOUNTAINS of New Hampshire; the latter through the lovely SACO VALLEY and CRAWFORD NOTCH, affording views of Grand Mountain Scenery second to none in America; also to the RANGELEY LAKES and waters of the Megantic Fish and Game Club, and to the SALMON WATERS of the PENOBSCOT, ST. JOHN, MIRAMICHI, and MATAPEDIA. Take trains from Boston & Maine Railroad Station in Boston or Worcester, connecting with Maine Central at Portland. Information furnished cheerfully on application to the General Passenger Agent at Portland.

PAYSON TUCKER, GENERAL MANAGER. F. E. BOOTHBY, GEN. PASS. AGENT.

Whenever the question of gauges or railway legislation came up, Lewiston, Auburn, Farmington, Bangor, and other cities on the broad gauge route were pitted against the "narrow gauge" towns of Augusta, Hallowell, Gardiner, Brunswick, Bath, and Skowhegan. One prominent legislator, Wyman Moor, a "Broad Gauge" man, who built the railroad between Waterville and Bangor, threatened to set up a battery between Kendall's Mills and Waterville and "blow the Somerset & Kennebec Railroad to the devil!" Ever since then the stretch of Maine Central Railroad between Waterville and Fairfield, originally a part of the Somerset & Kennebec, has been known as "Moor's Battery."

The battle of the gauges continued for thirty-five years. Leading the conversion from broad-gauge to standard gauge was the Androscoggin Railroad, between Leeds Junction and Farmington, which changed from broad to standard in 1861. This was not only the first broad gauge railroad in Maine to change to standard gauge, but it was also the first in

Advertisement describing the Maine Central's extensive connections to inland resorts, published in The Charming Inland Retreats of Maine, *Maine Central Railroad, c. 1890*

the United States. In 1870 the gauge of the Maine Central line between Waterville and Bangor was changed from broad to standard, and in 1871 that of the line between Waterville and Danville Junction was changed. The Grand Trunk converted its line to standard gauge in 1875.

Belfast & Moosehead Lake Railroad

During the "Battle of the Gauges," several important railway lines had been built or were under way. Notable among them was the thirty-four mile Belfast owned Belfast & Moosehead Lake Railroad, one of the very few city-owned railroads in the United States. If Belfast had realized its ambitions of a century or more ago, it would today be the seaport terminus for several railroad lines. The first company in Maine, and probably the first in the United States, to receive a charter for what was planned as an international railroad was the Belfast & Quebec Railroad, organized by Belfast citizens and chartered in 1836 for the purpose of building a railroad to the St. Lawrence River and diverting the traffic of that river to Penobscot Bay.

Belfast also had plans for railroads to Bangor, Newport, Moosehead Lake, Waterville, and Hallowell. The only one of those projects that materialized, however, was the Belfast & Moosehead Lake Railroad which had been chartered in 1853, and completed to Burnham Junction on the Maine Central in 1870. For some time the road was operated by the Maine Central under lease, but in recent years it has been operated independently.

European & North American Railroad

Now we come to one of the most interesting of all developments — the European & North American Railroad — a great name for a great plan promoted by none other than John A. Poor, who was by this time well established as the "Father of Maine Railroads." It is safe to say that no railroad in New England was the subject of more discussion, more speech-making, more publicity, and more attention on the part of legislators than the European & North American. John Poor established a newspaper in Portland to promote interest in it and to educate the public on its merits.

The European & North American was the only railway company in Maine to receive a state land grant. It was designed as a link in a great transcontinental chain of railroads that would reach from the easternmost tip of Nova Scotia to Boston, New York, Montreal, Detroit, Chicago, and on to the Pacific Ocean. Its promoters stressed the point that it would shorten the ocean trip between America and Europe and would cut two days from the transatlantic crossing time.

The company was chartered in 1850, but the project did not get under way until after the Civil War. General Veazie's road between Bangor & Old Town was purchased, and a broad gauge line was extended through Mattawamkeag and Vanceboro to St. John, New Brunswick. The last rail in the line was laid September 20, 1871, and on October 18th the President of the United States, Ulysses S. Grant, came by special train from Washington, and the Governor-General of Canada, Lord Lingard, came from Ottawa. Senators, Congressmen, governors, mayors, and other dignitaries gathered at the International Boundary at Vanceboro to celebrate the completion of this new and important artery of transportation - described by one speaker as "another link in the great chain binding the two nations in peace and friendship."

Although the European & North American Railroad never became the great route of travel to and from Europe visualized by its founders, it was for many years the main link between the United States and the Maritime Provinces of Canada. In 1882 that portion of the European & North American located in Maine was leased to the Maine Central, and since that time it has been operated as a part of the latter system. The Canadian portion, between Vanceboro and St. John, New Brunswick, is now a part of the Canadian Pacific.

Rash of Narrow Gaugers

Gauge standardization, begun in Maine in 1861, was completed on all important trunk lines in 1878, when the European & North American changed from broad to standard gauge. It had taken a long time but, even so, Maine was still eight years ahead of other parts of the country in gauge standardization. While this important change was taking place, however, a veritable rash of new narrow-gauge lines were chartered in Maine.

There was the Bucksport & Bangor Railroad, which could not make up its mind. It started out as a broad gauge road; then it changed to standard; two years later it went to three feet, and four years after that it switched back to standard. Four different gauges in seven years is probably a world's record!

CHAPTER I

"Grand International Railroad Opening, San Francisco, New York, Bangor, St. John, Halifax, The West Salutes the East," Vanceboro, Maine, October 18, 1871

Railway Development in Maine

Maine led all other states in the construction of two foot gauge railroads. In fact, common carrier railroads of two foot gauge were confined almost exclusively to Maine. In 1900, there were no fewer than eight two foot gauge roads in this state. The first to be built was the Sandy Stream Railroad between Farmington and Phillips. The first two foot gauge locomotive in America ran on this road in 1880.

The shortest two footer was the Kennebec Central, which ran for five miles between Randolph and the Soldiers' Home at Togus. The longest was the Sandy River & Rangeley Lakes Railroad, which was formed in 1908 from a consolidation of three narrow gauge lines comprising a total of about 102 miles of track.

One by one these two footers folded up, the last survivor, I believe, being the six mile line serving the slate quarries near Monson. When the Monson Railroad was built, the slate business was flourishing. Slate was used for roofing, tombstones, sinks, blackboards, and other purposes. But the slate business gradually died out, and the Monson Railroad died with it.

> These 2-footers were homey, friendly and leisurely little roads. The conductor was always glad to run errands for the folks living along the line - buying a spool of thread for Mrs. Stafford, delivering a note for Gil Moran, paying Sam Sleeper's taxes, fetching the mail for Aunt Mary Blake, or giving the editor at the county seat interesting bits of news for his paper. But once in a while even one of these little roads would make an enemy. For instance, there was Uncle Joe Foster who ran the gristmill on the Bridgton & Saco.
>
> When the road was being located he fought to have it run through his property. When he lost out he vowed he would "haul his freight to and from Japan with a rooster" before he would ship a pound of it over the Bridgton & Saco. And nothing could induce him to use the railroad after it was opened. [Source unidentified]

Bangor & Aroostook Railroad

During the 1880s there was widespread apprehension among Bangor and downstate business leaders concerning a situation which had been developing in Northern Maine. Railway lines extending northward from St. John and St. Andrews, New Brunswick, had projected two branch lines into Aroostook County. A branch of the New Brunswick

CHAPTER I

View of the Sandy River & Rangeley Lakes Railroad Station, Phillips, c. 1910

& Canada Railway was completed from Debec Junction to Houlton in 1869. This was the first railroad in Aroostook County. The Aroostook River Railroad, from the Aroostook Junction, on the same road in New Brunswick, reached Caribou in 1876 and Presque Isle in 1881, and the New Brunswick Railway paralleled the St. John River from Van Buren to Madawaska.

In 1885, the Canadian Pacific, expanding rapidly under Sir William Van Horn — the "Thunderbolt from Illinois" — began pushing across Maine from Megantic. Four years later the railroad was completed through Greenville and Brownville to a junction with the Maine Central at Mattawamkeag. Trackage rights over the Maine Central eastward from that point gave the Canadian Pacific a direct line from Montreal to St. John and Houlton. Another Canadian road from Quebec was seeking a line through the northern part of the state. All these developments underscored and aggravated the problem which had been discussed by Governor Israel Washburn as far back as 1861. In a message to the Maine Legislature, Governor Washburn stated that:

> The trade of the Aroostook, now rapidly increasing with the growth of its population, is in danger of being wholly diverted from this

state.... Already, much the larger part of it is carried on through channels of communication in a neighboring province, and without some effectual measures to arrest the present tendency of things, it will be wholly lost to us. With the needed facilities of transport within the state, its entire commerce ... would flow into the cities of Bangor and Calais.

Thirty years later in 1891, Governor Edwin C. Burleigh of Linneus, Aroostook's first native son and Ricker's first alumnus to become chief executive of this state, said in a message to the Legislature:

The state is now fairly supplied with railroad communication. There is, nevertheless, a field for further enterprise in this direction. Nowhere is this more apparent than in the great fertile county of Aroostook, whose varied products are now forced to seek a market over Canadian soil. A direct line over Maine territory, affording Aroostook a convenient outlet to the great markets of the country would give a mighty impulse to the development of the country and materially increase the prosperity of the whole state.

Out of this urgent need for a railroad having its roots in Maine and its interests in Maine, sprang the Bangor & Aroostook Railroad. It is safe to say that no single development more profoundly affected agricultural, industrial and social conditions in northern Maine than the coming of the Bangor & Aroostook. Indeed, the influence of the Bangor & Aroostook was and is felt throughout the state, because the traffic which originates on and is destined to points on this road helps to keep other railroads and other industries in New England busy and prosperous.

There were two logical routes for such a railroad. One was from Mattawamkeag, Danforth or some other point on the Maine Central through Houlton and Presque Isle; the other was from a junction with the Katahdin Iron Works in the vicinity of Brownville to Houlton, thence northward to the Aroostook Valley. The latter route, though more costly to build, would tap strategic water courses and the rich timber lands of the Schoodic-Millinocket-Grindstone region and would thus open new territory having great possibilities for industrial development. Finally a company was organized with the backing of Bangor capitalists, and in February, 1891, the Bangor & Aroostook Railroad Company

CHAPTER I

View of the Bangor & Piscataquis Railroad Station, West Cove, Moosehead Lake, c. 1884. This site became known as Greenville Junction after the International Railway of Maine (subsequently the Canadian Pacific) built a track that ran behind the station and across the middle of the photograph.

charter was signed by Governor Burleigh. Albert A. Burleigh, the Governor's brother and a farmer in Oakfield, became the first president. Franklin W. Cram, the superintendent of the Bangor & Katahdin Iron Works Railroad, became the general manager.

The building of the Bangor & Aroostook through the great north woods forms another epic story in Maine's railroad history. It is truly a story of rugged deeds performed by rugged men. In the winter of 1893 the road was completed to Houlton, and on New Year's Day, 1894 hundreds of eager spectators gathered along the railroad in Sherman, Crystal, Island Falls, Oakfield, Smyrna, Ludlow, New Limerick, and Houlton to cheer the first train from Bangor.

All Aroostook was taking on new life and a new outlook. Pushing northward, the rails reached Caribou and Fort Fairfield a year later, and the following year the Patten and Ashland branches were opened. In 1902 the Ashland branch was extended to Fort Kent. In 1905 the Bangor & Aroostook extended its line southward to Searsport, where a modern seaport terminal was opened, and in 1910 the railroad's network was completed by extensions from Squa Pan to Van Buren and thence to St. Francis.

RAILWAY DEVELOPMENT IN MAINE

Back cover illustration of *Vacationland*, Maine Central Railroad, 1932

CHAPTER I

"All A-Board for
'Vacationland,'"
Vacationland, Maine
Central Railroad, 1932

What has occurred in Aroostook within the memory of many of us furnishes a striking illustration of the value and the benefits of railway development. Before the Bangor & Aroostook was opened, some potatoes were grown but few were shipped out of the county because of the lack of transportation. By 1900 the annual crop had amounted to two million bushels. By 1910 it had jumped to eighteen million bushels. Production continued to increase until in recent years upwards of sixty million bushels have been shipped in a season. According to the United States Department of Agriculture, Aroostook County now produces 16 per cent — or about one-sixth — of the entire commercial potato crop of the United States, and the output of this county alone exceeds that of any state in the Union except Maine.

Maine's Railway System Today

Today, Maine's railway system embraces 1,860 miles of standard gauge road — enough to form a continuous line reaching from Houlton to Houston, Texas. These railroads represent an investment running into hundreds of millions of dollars. They employ thousands of workers, and they do a business of upwards of fifty million dollars a year.

From no fewer then 75 different railroads, Maine's railway system has evolved into six systems — the Boston & Maine, the Maine Central, the Bangor & Aroostook, the Belfast & Moosehead Lake, the Canadian Pacific, and the Canadian National — all so standardized in their operations, all working so closely and so harmoniously together to serve the people and the industries of this state that they might well be a single system.

The wooden railroads of long ago, the horse and ox-drawn cars, the coal-oil lamps and the wood burning stoves are no more. The narrow-gauge lines and the wood-burning locomotives have disappeared from the scene; the rate wars and gauge wars are happily things of the past. Even the steam locomotive and the old water tank are gradually disappearing from the scene.

Map of the "Mountain, Lake and Seashore Region of New England Reached by Boston and Maine Railroad and its Connections," appended to the company's promotional booklet titled *Summer in New England*, **1924**

CHAPTER I

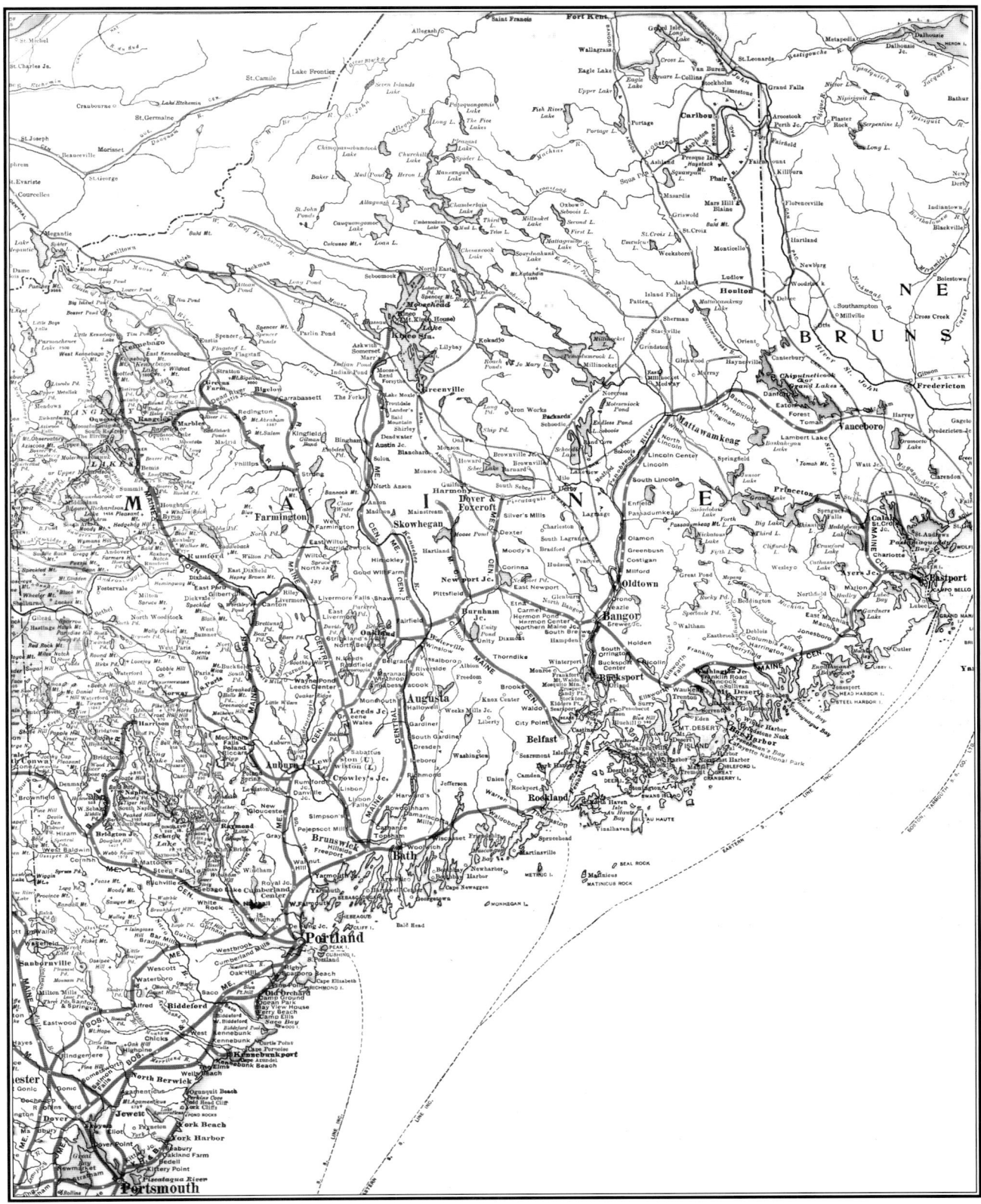

Bangor & Aroostook Railroad steam locomotive at the station in Oakfield, c. 1950

Postscript

Maine's railroad mileage reached its peak in 1924 when 2,379.39 miles of main line track were in active use. Over the succeeding decades nearly one-half of this system was abandoned, and at the beginning of the twenty-first century only 1,218.21 miles of rail are in operation (another 191.68 miles are still in place but not active). It is noteworthy, however, that three of the abandoned lines have been acquired by the Maine Department of Transportation, which has returned about 120 of its 300 miles of trackage to active operation through lease and operating agreements. In addition, the Department's long range planning foresees the return of limited passenger service over portions of this trackage, a development that will extend passenger rail connections beyond the projected restoration of AMTRAK service to Portland from Boston.

1   What is believed to be a three-quarter mile stretch of the original corridor beginning at Salmon Falls is still in active use. If this is in fact the same track (excepting the rails and ties), it would appear to be the oldest continually operated section of railroad in Maine. The earliest steam railroad corridor in continuous use is the Portland, Saco & Portsmouth line between Portland and North Berwick.

Editor's Note: The preceding overview of the history of railroads in Maine was presented by Carlton J. Corliss in the form of an address to the Ricker Classical Institute and Ricker College Alumni Association banquet, which was held in Houlton on June 8, 1953. Born in Crystal, Maine on April 29, 1888, Corliss graduated from Ricker in 1908, and at the time he gave his presentation was the manager of the Public Relations Department of the Association of American Railroads. According to his entry in the 1954 edition of *Who's Who in Railroading*, Corliss had a long and varied career in the railroad industry that included authorship of several articles and books on railway history, among which is *Main Line of Mid-America; the Story of the Illinois Central* (1950). Carlton Corliss retired to Tallahassee, Florida where he died in 1978. With only minor editing, the typescript manuscript, a copy of which is located at the Maine State Library, is presented as written by the author.

View of Union Station,
Maine Central Railroad,
Portland, c. 1915

CHAPTER II

Railroad Passenger Stations in Maine
AN OVERVIEW OF THEIR ARCHITECTURAL DEVELOPMENT
Roger G. Reed

The foremost historian of railroad passenger station architecture, Carol Meeks, observed that by the middle of the nineteenth century terminal buildings symbolically served the same purpose as the towered-gate houses of medieval cities in Europe. That is, they were the principal point of entry for most towns; the route for all visitors, be they kings or commoners. Long before automobiles and paved roads, many Americans traveled by land and relied on the passenger train as a means of long distance transportation. It was through the railroad stations that travelers often received their first impression of a community. Because of their importance as a means of transportation, railroad stations quickly evolved from functional structures to buildings that were richly ornamented in a variety of architectural styles. Support structures, such as engine houses, freight sheds, and water towers, were rarely embellished with ornament and serve to reinforce the fact that for most of the nineteenth century passenger stations represented the "gateway" for many towns. Their size and design, however, was dependent upon the corporate image selected by each railroad rather than the community itself.

The stations which best illustrate this in Maine were located in two of its largest cities: Portland and Bangor. The Maine Central Railroad's Union Station in Portland was designed in 1888 by Bradlee, Winslow & Wetherell of Boston. This magnificent Chateauesque style building was designed in the same spirit as the great hotels erected by the Canadian Pacific Railroad. On the opposite side of the Portland peninsula, the Grand Trunk Railway erected an equally monumental station in 1903. Bangor's large Richardsonian Romanesque-inspired station of 1905 was designed for the Maine Central by H. B. Fletcher and occupied a commanding location along the Penobscot River.

Although built in quite different architectural styles, these picturesque stations with their great clock towers were part of a tradition of passenger station design found throughout the country. Elsewhere in New England this pattern was represented by major depots such as the Park Street Station in Boston by Peabody & Stearns (1872-74), and Worcester's Union Station by Ware & Van Brunt (1875-77).

View of the Grand Trunk Railway Station, Portland, 1905

Many of the earliest train stations built in New England were simple structures that were often constructed directly over the tracks in the manner of a train shed (this practice appears to have been infrequent in Maine). Indeed, the housing of the engines rather than passengers seemed to be the principal concern in many locations. Thus, the train shed developed before the passenger depot, although the evolution of both types of structures occurred simultaneously. Crown Street Station in Liverpool, England, built in 1830, was the first major railroad station which combined both functions. It featured a two story Regency style rectangular building parallel to the tracks, which was joined to an attached gable roof train shed along one side. An early New England example of this type was in Lowell, where the Boston and Lowell "Car House" (as it is identified on original plans) of 1835 was similar, except for the station being in the Greek Revival style. Invariably, the train sheds had wooden trusses, although the side walls were frequently of masonry construction. For smaller depots where there was no train shed, the depot alongside the tracks often looked like an ordinary dwelling. During the 1840s the tendency was to combine the train shed and the depot into one large structure erected over the tracks. Prominent examples of this were the Old Colony Depot in Boston and the Eastern Railroad Depot in Salem, both designed by Gridley J. F. Bryant and dating from 1847. As engines became larger and terminals required more tracks, it became increasingly impractical to bridge the tracks using wood trusses exposed to the deleterious effects of sulfurous steam, not to mention the danger of fire.

For this reason train sheds evolved as separate structures, with cast iron replacing wood for the great roofs. The depots, whether or not the train shed was attached, were built using three basic plans. The most common was the "side house plan," in which the train pulled up alongside the station. A disadvantage of this where there were multiple tracks was that it required crossings to gain access to different lines. The "island plan" with its tracks on either side of the station reduced the problem of delays with trains traveling in different directions, but also required solutions to crossing tracks where there were multiple lines.

The "head house plan" proved to be the best solution for large operations as the station was built perpendicular to the tracks allowing for

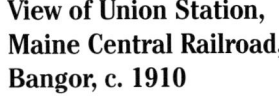

View of Union Station, Maine Central Railroad, Bangor, c. 1910

View of the Kennebec & Portland Railroad Station, Augusta, c. 1860

several lines to terminate behind the structure. Moreover, this arrangement reinforced the image of a station as a monumental architectural gateway when approached from within the city. In Maine only the Grand Trunk's Portland station employed a plan similar to the head house configuration.

The first train stations were multi-purpose buildings with passenger waiting rooms, baggage rooms and freight storage under one roof, although prosperous lines often built individual structures for passengers, even in rural areas. The stations themselves gradually offered improved facilities, such as separate men's and women's waiting rooms and ticket offices. Other rooms common even in small stations were telegraph and dispatcher's offices, baggage rooms, a freight office, and a station master's office. The largest stations also introduced restaurants, smoking rooms, and other amenities. In remote rural areas there could be a second floor with living quarters for the station master.

The station master's duties correspondingly grew more complex as he became responsible for tickets, baggage handling, dispatching and telegraphing, and — if a small station — freight. Baggage shipped by train included a variety of items ranging from trunks and pets, to coffins containing the deceased. Freight also became more varied and included parcels, machinery, and produce, not to mention entire houses ready for assembly from mail order firms such as Sears, Roebuck & Company.

While the exterior of a station could be ornamented in a variety of ways, wide overhanging eaves were essential to provide shelter from smoke and burning embers produced by the engines, as well as protection from the elements. Another common feature was the bay window for the station master and dispatcher's office. Located on the track side, this allowed him to keep watch of the tracks and the platform while tending to other duties. In the early 1900s, newly developed cement asbestos roofing shingles were introduced to reduce the incidence of fire.

Increased amenities in the stations became the norm after the Civil War as railroad lines engaged actively in the promotion of tourism. Indeed, when railroad travel lost its novelty as a means of transportation, the various lines competed to attract both passengers and investors. An architecturally prominent passenger station served both purposes, and a picturesque ornamental station gave each line a prominent landmark. By the early 1900s a uniform style, or at least standard paint colors, became a logical option for companies concerned with promoting their corporate identity.

The general trends outlined above were characteristic of the development of passenger stations in Maine. One of the earliest railroad lines in Maine, the Atlantic and St. Lawrence from Portland to Montreal, was leased by the Grand Trunk Railway. The stations built by that line illustrate many important features in the evolution of passenger station architecture. The first major railroad station building erected in Maine was constructed in Portland by the Grand Trunk in 1854. This replaced a simple vernacular building with a side house plan. The new station, one of the last of the great train-shed type stations, was erected over the tracks and was of masonry construction. The depot, designed by architect Francis Thompson of Montreal, was brick with a steep gable roof supported on wooden trusses. "Railroad Thompson," as he was known, began his career in England and acquired a considerable reputation for his design of railway structures.

During the mid-nineteenth century the Grand Trunk built a variety of smaller wooden stations along its line. As was typical of most railroads, stations of different sizes and different designs were erected at various stops, depending upon the requirements. For example, a station at Danville Junction, erected in 1864, was larger than most because it was situated at the junction of two major lines, the Grand Trunk and the

View of the Grand Trunk Railway Station, Danville Junction, c. 1911

Maine Central. For this reason the Gothic style structure included a large dining hall, as well as two waiting rooms, wash rooms, baggage rooms, and ticket and telegraph offices. It was built in an island plan with the Grand Trunk tracks on one side and the Maine Central tracks on the other. By 1911 the passenger traffic at Danville Junction had decreased, leading to the replacement of the old station with a smaller structure. The new station dispensed with the dining hall and had a smaller waiting room.

The Grand Trunk's early small wooden stations are represented by one structure that survives. This is the Gilead Station, which was moved and restored on its new site in Auburn. This building is noteworthy as it was apparently designed to be built in sections and moved by rail for assembly at its site. It was common for most railroad structures to be built of wood, and this was both because it was economical and because it allowed the railroad to use its own crews for maintenance.

The Grand Trunk was particularly important to the development of the Lewiston-Auburn area because it served as the primary transportation route over which French Canadian immigrants arrived to work in the area's large textile industry. The Grand Trunk's surviving Lewiston station is an important historic landmark in that city. Built by the Lewiston and Auburn Railroad in 1873 and leased to the Grand Trunk, its small size is testimony to the fact that it served as the terminus of a short line developed to handle the influx of immigrant labor from Canada.

CHAPTER II

Not surprisingly, its Italianate style detailing was quite modest. Another important survivor on this line dates from 1889 and is typical of the variety in station design during the last forty years of the nineteenth century. This is the South Paris station, a brick structure with a clipped gable roof and wide overhanging eaves. No information has come to light regarding the role of an architect in its design, or why the decision was made to construct it of brick.

The early twentieth century prosperity of the railroads resulted in the replacement of numerous stations in Maine, and the Grand Trunk was no exception. In 1903 its large nineteenth century terminal in Portland gave way to a grand Romanesque style building designed by the Detroit firm of Spier & Rohn. Built on an unusual plan with a center section and two angled wings facing the track ends, it was the closest Maine came to having a station with the head-house plan. With a tower in the center section facing the commercial district, it rivaled the more famous Union Station. The Grand Trunk station was demolished in 1966.

View of the Grand Trunk Railway Station, South Paris, c. 1895

43

The Grand Trunk passenger station in Yarmouth, built in 1906, exhibits common characteristics of small stations in Maine: a broad sweeping hip roof with wide over-hanging eaves supported on brackets, and an almost complete absence of all the varied forms of decorative millwork employed in the late nineteenth century. However, the Yarmouth station is architecturally distinguished through features such as the complexity of the roof configuration, the use of ashlar granite for the foundation, and the curved wall on one end of the building.

The Maine Central Railroad erected many of the most architecturally distinguished stations in Maine, including several in smaller towns. One of the earliest was the brick Italianate style station in Waterville, designed by the Boston firm of Bryant & Rogers. This 1872 masonry structure was a stylish local landmark similar to the firm's second Old Colony Railroad station in Boston of 1865. A smaller version of this station was built for the Maine Central in Augusta in 1866 from designs by Francis H. Fassett of Portland. This station was subsequently replaced in 1913 by a structure which was perhaps the most extraordinary station ever built in Maine. Designed by Robert C. Reamer, this polygonal-shaped station exhibited stylistic features that were influ-

View of the Maine Central Railroad Station, Waterville, c. 1875

View of the Maine Central Railroad Station, Augusta, c. 1870

enced by the Arts and Crafts movement and the work of Frank Lloyd Wright. It was a spectacular, architectural tour-de-force which was unlike any other depot built in Maine, if not New England. How this design came to be chosen is not known, but it further illustrates how railroad station designers were often allowed an extraordinary amount of artistic freedom.

The Maine Central Railroad maintained stylish stations in small rural areas as well. By using inexpensive woodwork produced by commercial sawmills, it was not difficult to create a great variety of elaborately ornamented styles for small buildings. As the Italianate style gave way to the Queen Anne, these changes in fashion were quickly reflected in new railroad buildings. This was not only true of larger lines, like the Maine Central and the Boston & Maine, but the small railroads, such as the York Harbor and Beach, and the Sandy River and its affiliated road.

RAILROAD PASSENGER STATIONS IN MAINE

Top: Construction photograph of the Maine Central Railroad Station, Augusta, 1913

Left: Exterior detail view of the Maine Central Railroad Station, Augusta, 1913

CHAPTER II

Right: View of the lobby,
Maine Central Railroad
Station, Augusta, 1913

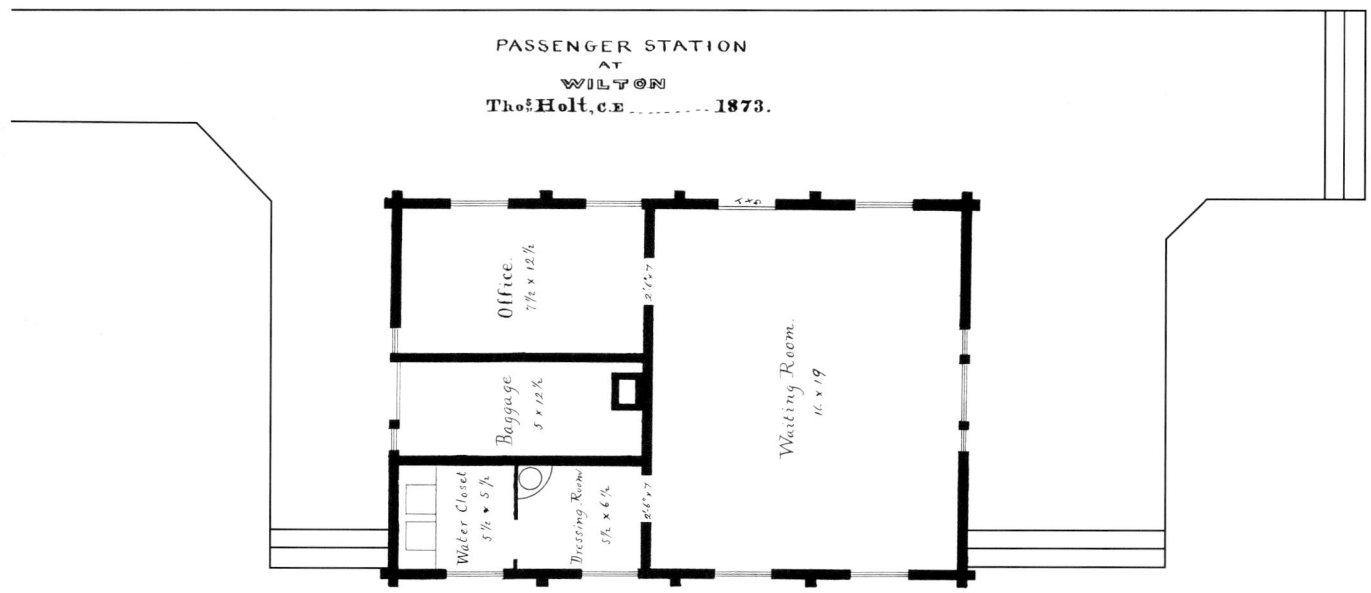

During the 1860s and 1870s the Maine Central employed an architect/engineer named Thomas Holt to design a series of small stations with decorative trim that reflected current architectural fashions. One of the documented designs by Holt was for the Wilton station, which was built in 1873. This small rectangular building features a gable roof with broad eaves supported by ornamented posts and brackets. The doors and windows are framed with architrave trim capped with cornices in the Italianate style. The basic amenities consisting of waiting room, station master's office, baggage room and toilet were included in this small station, which still survives at a different location. Larger Maine Central stations in the same style, such as Oakland and Cumberland Center, typically featured filigree ornament

Front elevation and floor plan drawings by Thomas Holt of the Maine Central Railroad Station, Wilton, 1873

CHAPTER II

MAINE CENTRAL RAILROAD STATION

Engraving of the Maine Central Railroad Station, Skowhegan, published in the *Skowhegan, Norridgewock, Madison, Anson, Solon & Bingham Souvenir*, 1908

on the eaves. The Cumberland Center station also supported a decorative ventilator tower, which is documented in elegantly drawn pen and ink drawings at the Maine Historical Society. Although unsigned, the design is probably the work of Thomas Holt. The Cumberland Center station contained a waiting room, ticket office, baggage room and separate toilets for men and women.

The use of standardized designs for smaller stations such as those built along the Grand Trunk and Maine Central railroads was not limited to these companies alone. In fact, each of the many individual railroad lines developed in Maine constructed stations which had relatively uniform characteristics yet were distinguishable from those of other lines. In some cases, these small railroads engaged the services of professionals

49

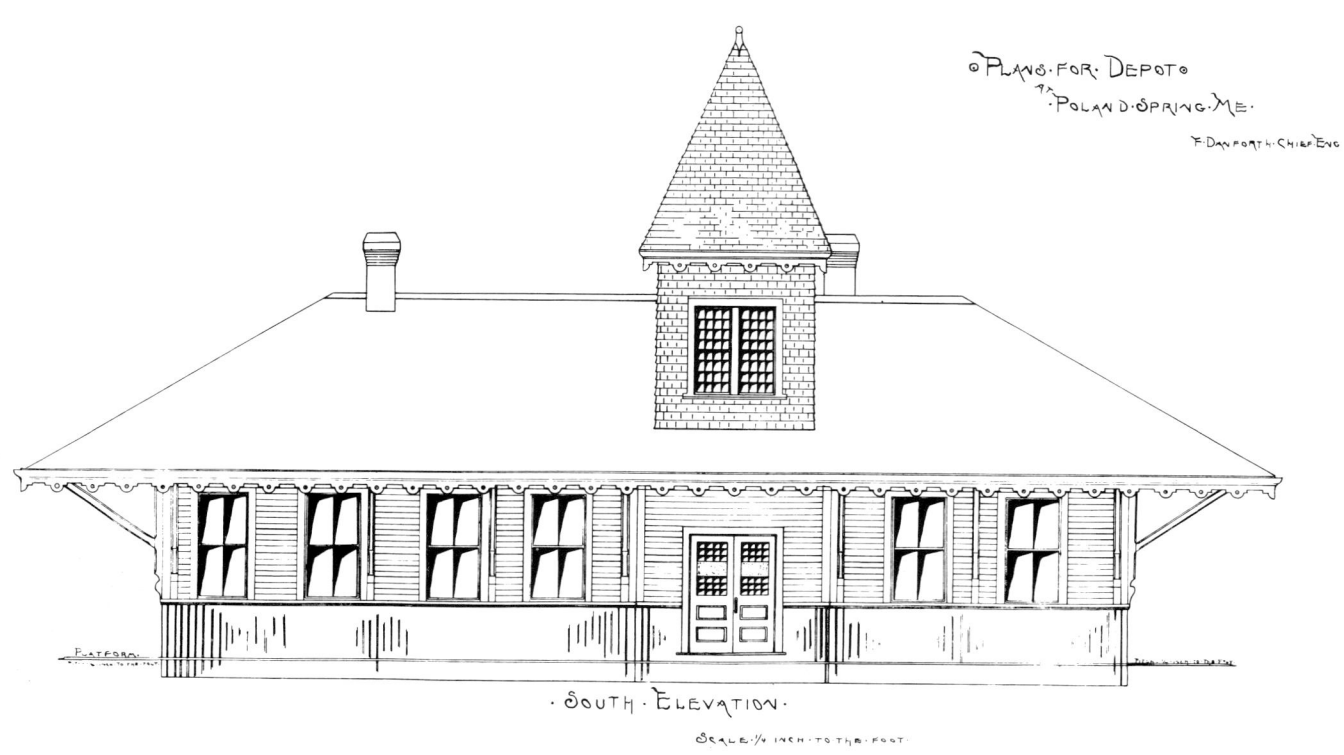

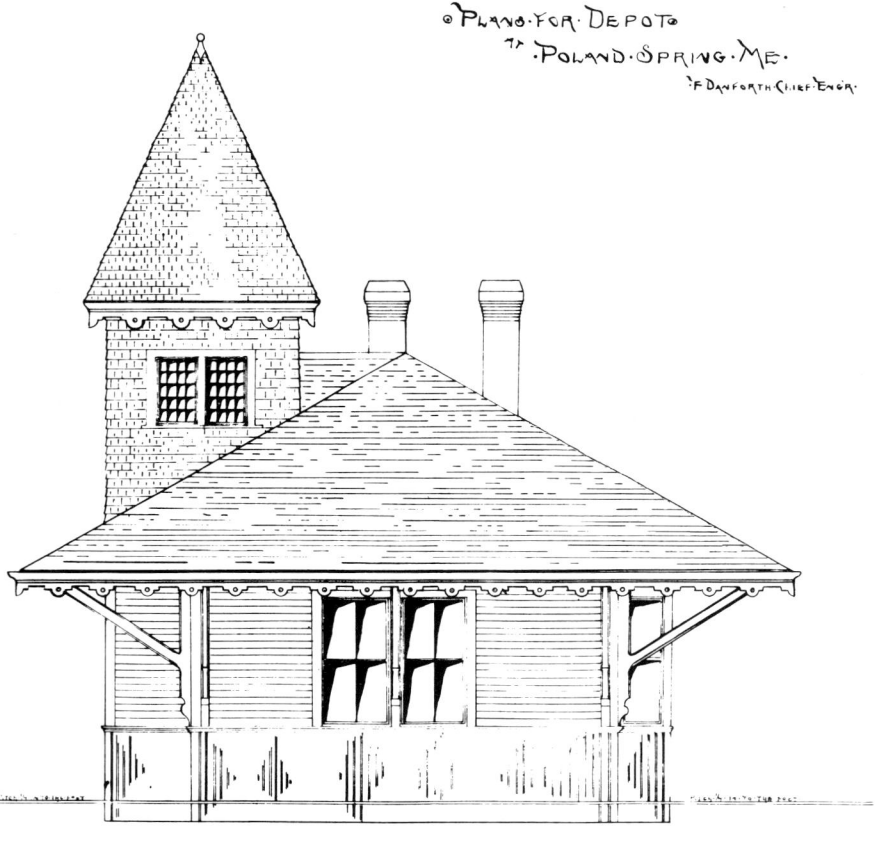

Top: Plans for Depot at Poland Springs, south elevation drawing by Frederick Danforth, Portland & Rumford Falls Railway, 1894

Bottom: Plans for Depot at Poland Springs, east elevation drawing by Frederick Danforth, Portland & Rumford Falls Railway, 1894

CHAPTER II

View of the Portland & Rumford Falls Railway Station, Poland Spring, c. 1900

to develop the designs that would distinguish their buildings from others. For example, architect E. E. Lewis and engineer Frederick Danforth (both of Gardiner) were commissioned to design the stations and buildings along the Portland & Rumford Falls Railway. The Canadian Pacific Railway developed a series of no less than twenty standard station designs, several of which utilize half timbering and stucco as decorative exterior finishes. The surviving station in Jackman closely resembles the half-timbered "CPR Standard No. 9 Station," although the plan has been reversed for this particular site. As a result of this individualized design process, surviving original stations erected by a particular line are readily identifiable from those which successor companies (such as the Maine Central which ultimately leased many of the small lines) may have subsequently built.

A few stations were designed in a style that was harmonious with local architecture. Two notable examples, both no longer standing, were at Bemis and Kennebunk Beach. The Bemis station was built of logs, which reflected the construction technique employed in sporting camps, and was presumably meant to appeal to the many visitors to western Maine who came to enjoy hunting and fishing. The station at Kennebunk Beach was a distinctive Shingle Style design that called to mind the

View of the Maine Central Railroad Station, Bemis, c. 1910

summer cottages on the coast. Another example of this type is the second Wells Beach station, which is a former Boston and Maine station that is still standing. With its large gambrel roof it was clearly meant to emulate the character of summer cottages on Maine's coast. The demolished Camp Ellis station drew its inspiration from the board and batten cottages in that area of York County.

A major change in the appearance of station design came at the turn of the century when, in both cities and towns, new structures were no longer designed in the spirit of gate-ways to a community. Efficiency became the watchword in the company reports of the time. As the responsibilities of the station master increased, the design of depots moved toward standardization. These stations tended to be smaller and with a lower profile, usually a hipped roof and no tower, although a gable roof might be employed.

An example of the gable roof variety, which is still extant, is the Maine Central station in Rockland, designed by Coolidge & Shattuck of Boston and erected in 1918. This building has little to distinguish itself from other civic buildings of the period except for clerestory windows to light the concourse and the shed roof to protect passengers on the track side. Another example of this change in station design by the same firm survives in Lewiston, where the Maine Central replaced its Queen Anne style upper station in 1918. The new structure is one story high with a broad hipped roof supporting several dormers. At one end the building is a full two stories. There are wide overhanging eaves supported on traditional brackets, but little in the way of ornamental detail. With its location behind several mills and off major thoroughfares, the modestly designed Lewiston station was never a prominent landmark. Yet its size is commensurate with the importance of Lewiston as a major urban center in Maine.

For smaller communities passenger stations continued to stand out as important landmarks. The best example in this regard is Maine Central's Gardiner station. Built in 1911 in a French Renaissance mode from a design by George Burnham of Portland, this building is one of the most elegant surviving stations in Maine. It is noteworthy for the manner in which granite for the foundation and fenestration is highlighted against

View of the Maine Central Railroad Station, Rockland, c. 1920

View of the Maine Central Railroad Station, Gardiner, c. 1912

the brick for the walls. Like so many of its contemporaries, it also has a characteristic broad hip roof supported on brackets, but the design stands out for its combination of materials, which are also employed for three prominent dormers.

Wood construction, of course, was much more common, and numerous modest examples include Freeport (now at the Boothbay Railway Village), Old Town and Lisbon Falls. Many of the stations from this period are documented in architectural drawings in the collections of the Maine Historical Society and the Maine Historic Preservation Commission. Unfortunately, no architect is identified on these plans, and they may have been the work of a talented draftsman working for the Maine Central Railroad.

The Bangor and Aroostook Railroad was a comparatively late addition to the state's rail network and its stations also appear to have followed the style established by the Maine Central for its smaller structures. Because this line was built in a relatively short period during the final phase of railroad construction in Maine, there is more of a consistency in station design. Two outstanding survivors are the recently restored stations in Oakfield and Fort Kent. A third is the neglected brick station at Fort Fairfield.

CHAPTER II

The last major passenger station erected in pre World War II Maine was for the Maine Central in Bath in 1941. Designed by company engineers, this station is a handsome Colonial Revival design. It symbolizes the end of an era in the architecture of railroad stations, for the postwar period witnessed the demise of passenger traffic in Maine.

As the foregoing discussion illustrates, there was an extraordinary variety in railroad station architecture in Maine during the nineteenth and early twentieth centuries. There appears to have been no pattern in the decision to use architects as opposed to company engineers. While the larger cities and towns had grand stations designed in elaborate picturesque styles by prominent architects, smaller towns also often had richly ornamented depots. However, even stations that were almost bereft of ornament were often the work of architects rather than company engineers.

Perspective sketch of the Proposed Station, Bath, *Bath Daily Times*, **August 21, 1941**

Railroad employees posed outside the Maine Central Railroad Station, Newport, c. 1900

CHAPTER III

A Catalogue of Railroad Stations
Sylvanus Doughty and Kirk F. Mohney

The following catalogue contains historical information and a photograph for each railroad station that was identified during the survey. Individual entries are organized alphabetically by town, and contain the name of the railroad which is believed to have built the station, its date of construction, the name of the architect or engineer who is credited with the design, and the building's current use. Although an equally valid case can be made to group the stations by railroad (as Robert F. Lord did in *Downeast Depots: Maine Railroad Stations in the Steam Era*), an alphabetical listing permits readers who are less familiar with Maine's historic railroad network to more easily locate extant stations in a particular town.

Documentary information has been obtained from a number of sources including references in newspapers and periodicals, original plans, published works, and the reports submitted by the railroads to the Bureau of Valuation of the Interstate Commerce Commission between 1914 and 1919. The Engineering Reports in particular are a valuable source of construction dates for all types of buildings and structures. The decision to use historic images of the stations — when available — was based on two factors: 1) they offer excellent documentation about the early if not original appearance of these buildings; and 2) they often provide a fascinating glimpse of the activities that centered around railroad stations when they were a focal point of community life.

ABBOT (MONSON JUNCTION)
Railroad: Monson & Athens
Date of Construction: c.1883
Current Use: Not in Use

ADDISON
Railroad: Washington County
Date of Construction: 1898
Current Use: Dwelling (moved from Columbia)

CHAPTER III

ALBION
Railroad: Wiscasset & Quebec
Date of Construction: c.1895
Current Use: Not in Use

AUBURN
Railroad: Grand Trunk
Date of Construction: 1851 (building on the left)
Current Use: Commercial (moved from Gilead)

A CATALOGUE OF RAILROAD STATIONS

AUGUSTA (RIVERSIDE)
Railroad: Maine Central
Date of Construction: 1911
Current Use: Dwelling

BATH
Railroad: Maine Central
Date of Construction: 1941
Engineer: W. F. Cummings, Chief Engineer
Current Use: Not in Use

CHAPTER III

BELFAST (CITY POINT)
Railroad: Maine Central
Date of Construction: 1871
Current Use: Private (moved from Corinna)

BELGRADE (NORTH)
Railroad: Maine Central
Date of Construction: 1901
Current Use: North Belgrade Baptist Church

A CATALOGUE OF RAILROAD STATIONS

BENTON (WEST)
Railroad: Maine Central
Date of Construction: 1886
Current Use: Dwelling

BIDDEFORD
Railroad: Boston & Maine
Date of Construction: 1870
Current Use: Social Hall

CHAPTER III

BINGHAM (HEIGHTS)
Railroad: Somerset Railway
Date of Construction: 1909
Current Use: Dwelling

BOOTHBAY
Railroad: Maine Central
Date of Construction: 1912
Current Use: Museum (moved from Freeport)

A CATALOGUE OF RAILROAD STATIONS

BOOTHBAY
Railroad: Belfast & Moosehead Lake
Date of Construction: 1871
Current Use: Museum (moved from Thorndike)

BROOKS
Railroad: Belfast & Moosehead Lake
Date of Construction: 1881/1896
Current Use: Railroad

CHAPTER III

BUCKSPORT
Railroad: Eastern Maine Shore Line (combination)
Date of Construction: 1876
Current Use: Museum

CALAIS
Railroad: Washington County (combination)
Date of Construction: 1898
Current Use: Commercial

A CATALOGUE OF RAILROAD STATIONS

CANTON
Railroad: Portland & Oxford Central
Date of Construction: 1872
Current Use: Lodge

CARIBOU
Railroad: Bangor & Aroostook
Date of Construction: 1929
Current Use: Commercial

CHAPTER III

CARRABASSETT VALLEY (BIGELOW)
Railroad: Franklin & Megantic
Date of Construction: c.1900
Current Use: Not in Use

CHERRYFIELD
Railroad: Washington County
Date of Construction: 1898
Current Use: Not in Use

A CATALOGUE OF RAILROAD STATIONS

CHINA (SOUTH)
Railroad: Wiscasset & Quebec
Date of Construction: c.1895
Current Use: Dwelling

DANFORTH
Railroad: European & North American
Date of Construction: 1871
Current Use: Railroad

CHAPTER III

ELLSWORTH
Railroad: Maine Central
Date of Construction: 1928
Engineer: B. T. Wheeler, Chief Engineer
Current Use: Commercial

FARMINGTON
Railroad: Maine Central
Date of Construction: 1900
Current Use: Commercial

A CATALOGUE OF RAILROAD STATIONS

FARMINGTON (WEST)
Railroad: Maine Central
Date of Construction: 1902
Current Use: Post Office (pending)

FORT FAIRFIELD
Railroad: Bangor & Aroostook
Date of Construction: 1894
Current Use: Not in Use

CHAPTER III

FORT FAIRFIELD
Railroad: Canadian Pacific
Date of Construction: 1889
Current Use: Museum (moved)

FORT KENT
Railroad: Fish River
Date of Construction: 1902
Current Use: Museum

A CATALOGUE OF RAILROAD STATIONS

FRENCHVILLE
Railroad: Bangor & Aroostook
Date of Construction: 1910
Current Use: Museum

GARDINER
Railroad: Maine Central
Date of Construction: 1911
Architect: George Burnham of Portland
Current Use: Not in Use

CHAPTER III

GORHAM
Railroad: Boston & Maine
Date of Construction: 1887
Current Use: Commercial

HARTFORD (EAST SUMNER)
Railroad: Portland & Rumford Falls
Date of Construction: 1894
Architect/Civil Engineer: E.E. Lewis, architect and Frederick Danforth, engineer, both of Gardiner
Current Use: Dwelling

A CATALOGUE OF RAILROAD STATIONS

JACKMAN
Railroad: Canadian Pacific
Date of Construction: 1910/1927
Current Use: Railroad

JAY
Railroad: Maine Central
Date of Construction: 1873
Architect: Thomas Holt of Portland
Current Use: Commercial (moved from Wilton)

CHAPTER III

KENNEBUNK
Railroad: Boston & Maine
Date of Construction: 1884
Current Use: Commercial

KENNEBUNK (PARSONS)
Railroad: Boston & Maine
Date of Construction: 1883
Current Use: Residential

A CATALOGUE OF RAILROAD STATIONS

KENNEBUNKPORT
Railroad: Boston & Maine
Date of Construction: 1883
Current Use: Commercial

KINGFIELD
Railroad: Franklin & Megantic
Date of Construction: after 1923
Current Use: Commercial

CHAPTER III

KITTERY (POINT)
Railroad: York Harbor & Beach
Date of Construction: c.1887
Current Use: Dwelling

LAGRANGE (SOUTH)
Railroad: Bangor & Aroostook
Date of Construction: 1902
Current Use: Dwelling

A CATALOGUE OF RAILROAD STATIONS

LEBANON (EAST)
Railroad: Portland & Rochester
Date of Construction: c.1881
Architect/Civil Engineer:
Current Use: Dwelling

LEWISTON
Railroad: Grand Trunk
Date of Construction: 1885
Architect/Civil Engineer:
Current Use:

CHAPTER III

LEWISTON (UPPER)
Railroad: Maine Central
Date of Construction: 1917
Architect: Coolidge & Shattuck of Boston
Current Use: Commercial

LINCOLN
Railroad: Maine Central
Date of Construction: 1901
Current Use: Railroad

A CATALOGUE OF RAILROAD STATIONS

LISBON (FALLS)
Railroad: Maine Central
Date of Construction: 1909
Current Use: Commercial

LITTLE SQUAW TOWNSHIP (GREENVILLE JUNCTION)
Railroad: Canadian Pacific
Date of Construction: 1889
Current Use: Not in Use

CHAPTER III

MACHIAS
Railroad: Washington County
Date of Construction: 1898
Current Use: Commercial

MADISON
Railroad: Somerset (combination)
Date of Construction: 1876

MECHANIC FALLS
Railroad: Maine Central
Date of Construction: 1906
Current Use: Commercial

MINOT (WEST)
Railroad: Portland & Rumford Falls
Date of Construction: 1896
Architect/Civil Engineer: E.E. Lewis, architect and Frederick Danforth, engineer, both of Gardiner
Current Use: Dwelling

CHAPTER III

MONSON
Railroad: Monson & Athens (combination)
Date of Construction: c.1881
Current Use: Storage

NEWCASTLE
Railroad: Knox & Lincoln
Date of Construction: c.1871
Current Use: Commercial

A CATALOGUE OF RAILROAD STATIONS

NORRIDGEWOCK
Railroad: Somerset (combination)
Date of Construction: 1876
Current Use: Storage

NORTH BERWICK
Railroad: Boston & Maine
Date of Construction: 1907
Current Use: Commercial

CHAPTER III

OAKFIELD
Railroad: Bangor & Aroostook
Date of Construction: 1912
Current Use: Museum

OLD TOWN
Railroad: Maine Central
Date of Construction: 1904
Current Use: Commercial

A CATALOGUE OF RAILROAD STATIONS

ORONO
Railroad: European & North American
Date of Construction: 1876
Current Use: Dwelling

PARIS (SOUTH)
Railroad: Grand Trunk
Date of Construction: 1888-89
Current Use: Commercial

CHAPTER III

PHILLIPS
Railroad: Sandy River
Date of Construction: c.1879
Current Use: Social Hall

PHILLIPS
Railroad: Phillips & Rangeley
Date of Construction: c.1890
Current Use: Museum (moved from Madrid (Sanders))

A CATALOGUE OF RAILROAD STATIONS

PITTSFIELD
Railroad: Maine Central
Date of Construction: 1886
Current Use: Museum

POLAND
Railroad: Maine Central
Date of Construction: 1901
Current Use: Dwelling

CHAPTER III

PRESQUE ISLE
Railroad: Bangor & Aroostook
Date of Construction: c.1894
Current Use: Commercial

PRINCETON
Railroad: Maine Central
Date of Construction: 1905
Current Use: Airport

A CATALOGUE OF RAILROAD STATIONS

PRINCETON
Railroad: Maine Central
Date of Construction: 1901
Current Use: Dwelling (moved from Woodland)

RANGELEY (MARBLES)
Railroad: Phillips & Rangeley
Date of Construction: 1906
Current Use: Dwelling

CHAPTER III

ROCKLAND
Railroad: Maine Central
Date of Construction: 1917
Architect: Coolidge & Shattuck of Boston
Current Use: Commercial

ROXBURY
Railroad: Rumford Falls & Rangeley Lakes
Date of Construction: c.1894
Architect/Civil Engineer: E. E. Lewis, architect and Frederick Danforth, civil engineer, both of Gardiner
Current Use: Dwelling

A CATALOGUE OF RAILROAD STATIONS

SCARBOROUGH
Railroad: Boston & Maine
Date of Construction: 1906
Current Use: Commercial

SEARSPORT
Railroad: Bangor & Aroostook
Date of Construction: 1905
Current Use: Not in Use

CHAPTER III

THE FORKS PLANTATION (TROUTDALE, FORMERLY MOSQUITO)
Railroad: Somerset Railway Co.
Date of Construction: c. 1906
Current Use: Camp

THOMASTON
Railroad: Knox & Lincoln
Date of Construction: 1795 (as a dwelling)
Current Use: Museum

A CATALOGUE OF RAILROAD STATIONS

UNITY
Railroad: Belfast & Moosehead Lake
Date of Construction: 1891
Current Use: Railroad

VANCEBORO
Railroad: Maine Central
Date of Construction: 1906
Current Use: Railroad

CHAPTER III

WELLS
Railroad: Boston & Maine
Date of Construction: 1879
Current Use: Museum (moved from South Berwick (Cummings))

WELLS
Railroad: York Harbor & Beach
Date of Construction: 1885
Current Use: Not in Use (moved from York (Long Beach))

A CATALOGUE OF RAILROAD STATIONS

WELLS (BEACH)
Railroad: Boston & Maine
Date of Construction: 1906
Current Use: Dwelling

WELLS (ELMS)
Railroad: Boston & Maine
Date of Construction: 1879
Current Use: Commercial

CHAPTER III

WINDHAM (NEWHALL)
Railroad: Maine Central
Date of Construction: 1889
Current Use: Storage

WINDHAM (SOUTH)
Railroad: Maine Central
Date of Construction: 1909
Current Use: Storage

WINTERPORT
Railroad: Bangor & Aroostook
Date of Construction: 1905
Current Use: Not in Use

YARMOUTH
Railroad: Grand Trunk
Date of Construction: 1906
Current Use: Commercial

CHAPTER III

YORK (HARBOR)
Railroad: Boston & Maine
Date of Construction: 1900
Current Use: Dwelling

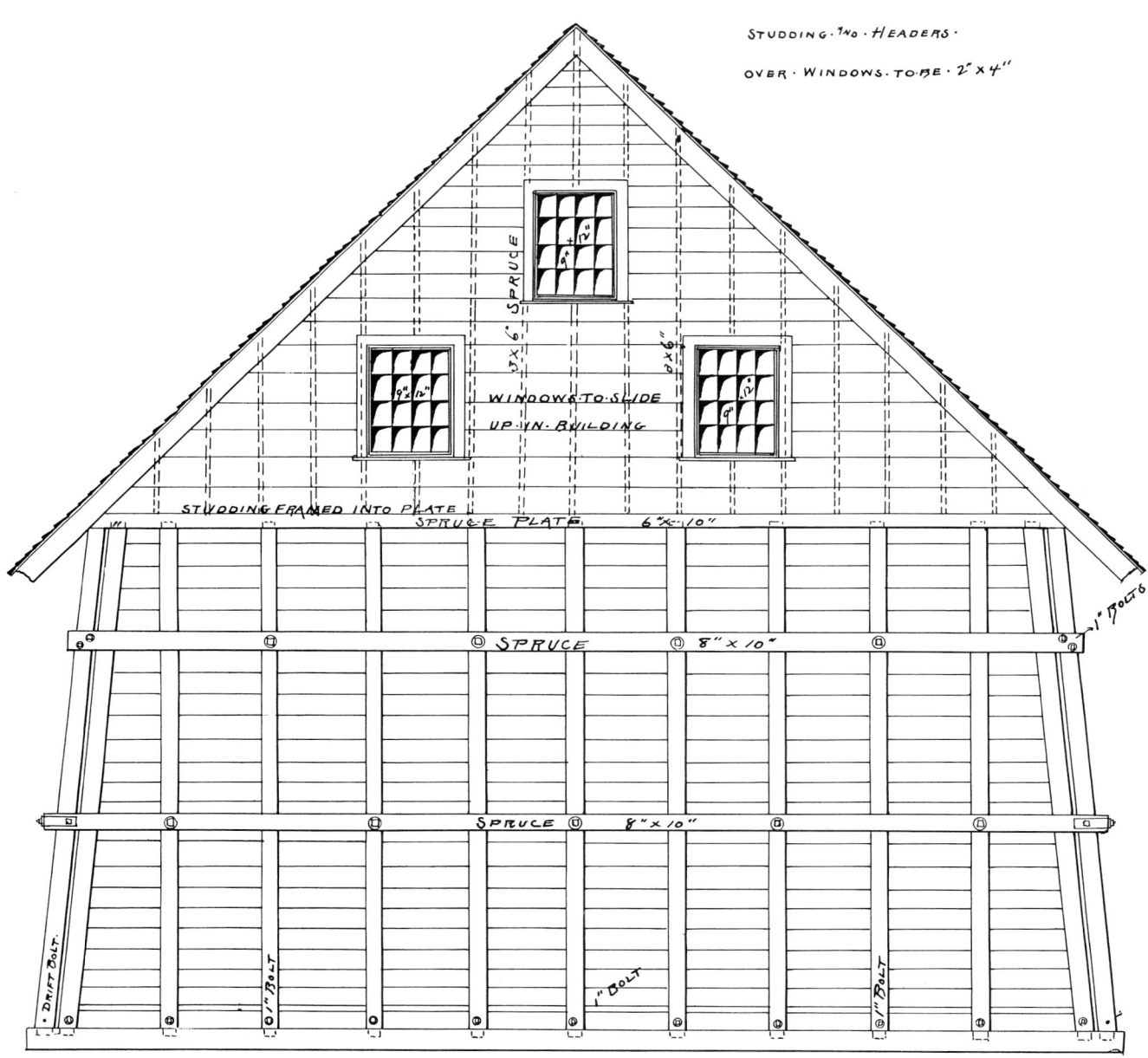

North elevation drawing for a Coal Shed at Rumford Falls, Portland & Rumford Falls Railway, April 29, 1896

CHAPTER IV

A Catalogue of Railroad Buildings
Sylvanus Doughty and Kirk F. Mohney

The Catalogue of Railroad Buildings includes all other buildings and structures that were identified during the survey. In similar fashion to the Catalogue of Railroad Stations, the entries are organized alphabetically by town rather than by the name of the associated railroad. This will allow the reader to more easily find the buildings in a particular geographical area. Each entry lists the original railroad company that is thought to have constructed the building, and gives a date of construction where one has been ascertained from the Interstate Commerce Commission valuation reports. Care has been taken in the use of this information to ascribe dates of construction only to those buildings that are referenced in the reports, and whose existing architectural characteristics are compatible with a pre-1920 time frame. Nonetheless, it is important to recognize that many of the smaller buildings were highly mobile, and that railroads did occasionally relocate them. This practice introduces a measure of uncertainty about the reliability of dates of construction for some types of buildings, although the fact remains that many others remain on their original sites. Future research in railroad company records may yield more information about which of these facilities was moved and when.

The nomenclature used in the catalogue is based on the descriptions and definitions in Walter G. Berg's reference book titled *Buildings and Structures of American Railroads* (1911), as well as the classifications that appear in the valuation reports. A comparison of these two sources indicates that the terms used to describe particular types of railroad buildings was relatively consistent among railroad companies in the United States.

A CATALOGUE OF RAILROAD BUILDINGS

ABBOT (MONSON JUNCTION)
Building Type: Turntable
Railroad: Monson & Athens
Current Use: Abandoned

ALFRED
Building Type: Freight House
Railroad: Boston & Maine
Date of Construction: 1846
Current Use: Commercial

ANSON (NORTH)
Building Type: Freight House
Railroad: Somerset Railway
Date of Construction: 1901
Current Use: Not in use

AUBURN
Building Type: Freight House
Railroad: Maine Central
Date of Construction: 1913
Current Use: Commercial

AUBURN (DANVILLE JUNCTION)
Building Type: Section Tool House
Railroad: Maine Central
Date of Construction: 1888
Current Use: Railroad

BALD MOUNTAIN TOWNSHIP (BAKERS)
Building Type: Dwelling House (2)
Railroad: Somerset Railway Co.
Date of Construction: 1909
Current Use: Residential

BALDWIN (EAST)
Building Type: Freight House
Railroad: Maine Central
Date of Construction: 1898
Current Use: Garage

BANCROFT
Building Type: Section Tool House
Railroad: Canadian Pacific
Date of Construction: 1896
Current Use: Not in use

BATH
Building Type: Freight House
Railroad: Maine Central
Date of Construction: 1901
Current Use: Commercial

BELFAST
Building Type: Engine House (radial)
Railroad: Belfast & Moosehead Lake
Date of Construction: 1864
Current Use: Railroad

Building Type: Freight House
Railroad: Belfast & Moosehead Lake
Date of Construction: 1881
Current Use: Railroad

Building Type: Car House (2)
Railroad: Belfast & Moosehead Lake
Current Use: Railroad

Building Type: Turntable (manual)
Railroad: Belfast & Moosehead Lake
Current Use: Railroad

BELFAST (CITY POINT)
Building Type: Section Tool House
Railroad: Belfast & Moosehead Lake
Current Use: Not in use

BOOTHBAY (RAILWAY VILLAGE)
Building Type: Section Tool House
Railroad: Maine Central
Date of Construction: 1901
Current Use: Museum (moved from Bath)

Building Type: Signal Tower
Railroad: Maine Central
Current Use: Museum (moved from Bath)

Building Type: Section Tool House
Railroad: Maine Central
Date of Construction: 1891
Current Use: Museum (moved from Brunswick)

CHAPTER IV

Interior view of the train shed, Union Station, Maine Central Railroad, Bangor, 1908

Building Type: Signal Tower
Railroad: Maine Central
Current Use: Museum (moved from Lewiston)

Building Type: Watchman's Shanty
Railroad: Maine Central
Date of Construction: 1896
Current Use: Museum (moved from Oakland)

Building Type: Watchman's Shanty
Railroad: Maine Central
Current Use: Museum (moved from Portland)

Building Type: Section Tool House
Railroad: Maine Central
Date of Construction: 1902
Current Use: Museum (moved from South Gardiner)

Building Type: Watchman's Shanty
Railroad: Maine Central
Current Use: Museum (moved from South Warren)

Building Type: Section Tool House
Railroad: Maine Central
Date of Construction: 1886
Current Use: Museum (moved from Wiscasset)

Building Type: Section Tool House
Railroad: Maine Central
Date of Construction: 1904
Current Use: Museum (moved from Woolwich)

BOWDOINHAM
Building Type: Freight House
Railroad: Maine Central
Date of Construction: 1882
Current Use: Storage

A CATALOGUE OF RAILROAD BUILDINGS

Railroad employees posed alongside the Maine Central Railroad Freight Office, Augusta, c. 1910

BROWNVILLE (JUNCTION)
Building Type: Hydrant House
Railroad: Canadian Pacific
Current Use: Railroad

Building Type: Section Tool House
Railroad: Canadian Pacific
Current Use: Railroad

Building Type: Dwelling House (3)
Railroad: Canadian Pacific
Date of Construction: 1919
Current Use: Residential

BRUNSWICK
Building Type: Engine House (radial)
Railroad: Maine Central
Date of Construction: 1873, 1889, 1904
Current Use: Storage

CALAIS
Building Type: Engine House
Railroad: Maine Central
Current Use: Not in use

CALAIS (MILLTOWN)
Building Type: Engine House (radial)
Railroad: Maine Central
Date of Construction: 1911
Current Use: Commercial

Building Type: Turntable (electric)
Railroad: Maine Central
Current Use: Railroad

CALAIS (ST. CROIX JUNCTION)
Building Type: Watchman's Shanty
Railroad: Maine Central
Date of Construction: 1905
Current Use: Not in use

CHAPTER IV

CARIBOU
Building Type: Coaling Station
Railroad: Bangor & Aroostook
Current Use: Commercial

Building Type: Engine House (radial)
Railroad: Bangor & Aroostook
Date of Construction: 1896, 1912
Current Use: Commercial

Building Type: Turntable (manual)
Railroad: Bangor & Aroostook
Current Use: Not in use

CHINA (WEEKS MILLS)
Building Type: Freight House
Railroad: Wiscasset & Quebec
Date of Construction: c.1895
Current Use: Not in use

DANFORTH
Building Type: Freight House
Railroad: European & North American
Date of Construction: 1871
Current Use: Not in use

Building Type: Section Tool House
Railroad: Canadian Pacific
Date of Construction: 1896
Current Use: Railroad

DEXTER
Building Type: Freight House
Railroad: Maine Central
Date of Construction: 1891
Current Use: Commercial

DOVER-FOXCROFT
Building Type: Engine House
Railroad: Maine Central
Date of Construction: 1891
Current Use: Commercial

Building Type: Freight House
Railroad: Maine Central
Date of Construction: 1892
Current Use: Commercial

ELLIOTSVILLE TOWNSHIP (BODFISH)
Building Type: Section House
Railroad: Canadian Pacific
Date of Construction: 1891
Current Use: Railroad

ELLSWORTH
Building Type: Section Tool House
Railroad: Maine Central
Date of Construction: 1884
Current Use: Not in use

FARMINGTON
Building Type: Freight House
Railroad: Maine Central
Date of Construction: 1868
Current Use: Commercial

FOREST TOWNSHIP
Building Type: Section Tool House
Railroad: Canadian Pacific
Date of Construction: 1896
Current Use: Not in use

FORT KENT
Building Type: Engine House
Railroad: Bangor & Aroostook
Date of Construction: 1902
Current Use: Railroad

FRANKFORT
Building Type: Freight House
Railroad: Bangor & Aroostook
Date of Construction: 1905
Current Use: Not in use

FREEPORT
Building Type: Section Tool House
Railroad: Maine Central
Date of Construction: 1911
Current Use: Not in use

FRENCHVILLE
Building Type: Freight House
Railroad: Bangor & Aroostook
Date of Construction: 1910
Current Use: Commercial

A CATALOGUE OF RAILROAD BUILDINGS

Building Type: Water Station
Railroad: Bangor & Aroostook
Date of Construction: 1910
Current Use: Museum

FRYEBURG
Building Type: Freight House
Railroad: Portland & Ogdensburg
Date of Construction: 1871
Current Use: Commercial

GARDINER
Building Type: Freight House
Railroad: Maine Central
Date of Construction: 1890
Current Use: Storage, partially demolished

GREENE
Building Type: Section Tool House
Railroad: Maine Central
Current Use: Not in use

HALLOWELL
Building Type: Freight House
Railroad: Maine Central
Date of Construction: 1892
Current Use: Not in use

HANCOCK (WASHINGTON JUNCTION)
Building Type: Section Tool House
Railroad: Maine Central
Date of Construction: 1886
Current Use: Not in use

HERMON (NORTHERN MAINE JUNCTION)
Building Type: Coaling Station
Railroad: Bangor & Aroostook
Current Use: Not in use

Building Type: Coal House
Railroad: Bangor & Aroostook
Current Use: Railroad

Building Type: Engine House (radial)
Railroad: Bangor & Aroostook
Date of Construction: 1907
Current Use: Railroad

Building Type: Turntable (electric)
Railroad: Bangor & Aroostook
Current Use: Railroad

Building Type: Tool House
Railroad: Maine Central
Current Use: Railroad

Building Type: Coaling Station
Railroad: Maine Central
Current Use: Not in use

Building Type: Office Building
Railroad: Maine Central
Current Use: Railroad

HOULTON
Building Type: Car Shed
Railroad: Bangor & Aroostook
Date of Construction: 1902
Current Use: Railroad

Building Type: Engine House (radial)
Railroad: Bangor & Aroostook
Date of Construction: 1912
Current Use: Commercial

Building Type: Turntable (electric)
Railroad: Bangor & Aroostook
Current Use: Not in use

ISLAND FALLS
Building Type: Freight House
Railroad: Bangor & Aroostook
Date of Construction: 1893
Current Use: Commercial

JACKMAN
Building Type: Freight House
Railroad: Canadian Pacific
Date of Construction: 1906
Current Use: Commercial

Building Type: Section Tool House (2)
Railroad: Canadian Pacific
Current Use: Railroad

CHAPTER IV

View of the Forest Avenue Gate House, Maine Central Railroad, Portland, c. 1963; photo, John Calvin Stevens II

LAGRANGE (SOUTH)
Building Type: Freight House
Railroad: Bangor & Piscataquis
Date of Construction: 1870
Current Use: Not in use

LISBON (FALLS)
Building Type: Section Tool House
Railroad: Maine Central
Date of Construction: 1901
Current Use: Commercial

Building Type: Freight House
Railroad: Maine Central
Date of Construction: 1909
Current Use: Not in use

LIVERMORE FALLS
Building Type: Engine House
Railroad: Maine Central
Date of Construction: 1897
Current Use: Railroad

MACHIAS
Building Type: Freight House
Railroad: Washington County
Date of Construction: 1898
Current Use: Not in use

MECHANIC FALLS
Building Type: Freight House
Railroad: Grand Trunk
Date of Construction: 1883
Current Use: Not in use

A CATALOGUE OF RAILROAD BUILDINGS

View of the Read Street Crossing Gate House, Maine Central Railroad, Portland, c. 1910

Building Type: Freight House
Railroad: Rumford Falls & Buckfield
Date of Construction: 1876
Current Use: Commercial

MILLINOCKET
Building Type: Coaling Station
Railroad: Bangor & Aroostook
Current Use: Not in use

Building Type: Coal House
Railroad: Bangor & Aroostook
Current Use: Not in use

Building Type: Engine House (radial)
Railroad: Bangor & Aroostook
Date of Construction: 1907
Current Use: Railroad

Building Type: Turntable (electric)
Railroad: Bangor & Aroostook
Current Use: Railroad

MILO
Building Type: Freight House
Railroad: Bangor & Aroostook
Date of Construction: 1902
Current Use: Not in use

MILO (DERBY)
Building Type: Car Repair and Paint Shop
Railroad: Bangor & Aroostook
Date of Construction: 1905
Current Use: Railroad

Building Type: Machine and Erecting Shop
Railroad: Bangor & Aroostook
Date of Construction: 1905
Current Use: Railroad

Building Type: Coaling Station
Railroad: Bangor & Aroostook
Date of Construction: c.1905
Current Use: Not in use

CHAPTER IV

Building Type: Lumber Shed
Railroad: Bangor & Aroostook
Date of Construction: 1908
Current Use: Railroad

Building Type: Storehouse and Office
Railroad: Bangor & Aroostook
Date of Construction: 1906
Current Use: Railroad

Building Type: Carpenter Shop and Planing Mill
Railroad: Bangor & Aroostook
Date of Construction: 1905
Current Use: Railroad

Building Type: Engine House (radial)
Railroad: Bangor & Aroostook
Date of Construction: c.1905
Current Use: Railroad

Building Type: Transfer Table (electric)
Railroad: Bangor & Aroostook
Date of Construction: 1905
Current Use: Railroad

Building Type: Turntable (electric)
Railroad: Bangor & Aroostook
Date of Construction: c.1905
Current Use: Railroad

MINOT (WEST)
Building Type: Freight House
Railroad: Portland & Rumford Falls
Date of Construction: 1892
Current Use: Residential

MONMOUTH
Building Type: Freight House
Railroad: Maine Central
Date of Construction: 1894
Current Use: Commercial

NEWCASTLE
Building Type: Freight House
Railroad: Maine Central
Date of Construction: 1896
Current Use: Not in use

NORTH BERWICK
Building Type: Watchman's Shanty
Railroad: Boston & Maine
Date of Construction: 1908
Current Use: Commercial

OAKFIELD
Building Type: Coaling Station
Railroad: Bangor & Aroostook
Current Use: Not in use

OAKLAND
Building Type: Freight House
Railroad: Maine Central
Date of Construction: 1901
Current Use: Railroad

OLD TOWN
Building Type: Freight House
Railroad: Maine Central
Date of Construction: 1905
Current Use: Railroad

PATTEN
Building Type: Freight House
Railroad: Patten & Sherman
Date of Construction: 1896
Current Use: Not in use

PHILLIPS
Building Type: Car Repair Shop
Railroad: Sandy River
Date of Construction: 1901
Current Use: Not in use

Building Type: Section Tool House
Railroad: Sandy River
Current Use: Museum

Building Type: Section House
Railroad: Sandy River
Current Use: Museum

Building Type: Freight House
Railroad: Phillips & Rangeley
Date of Construction: 1895
Current Use: Museum (moved from Sanders)

A CATALOGUE OF RAILROAD BUILDINGS

PORTLAND
EAST DEERING
Building Type: Boiler Room
Railroad: Grand Trunk
Date of Construction: 1902
Current Use: Commercial

Building Type: Engine House (radial)
Railroad: Grand Trunk
Date of Construction: 1902, c.1920
Current Use: Commercial

Building Type: Office and Store Room
Railroad: Grand Trunk
Date of Construction: 1901
Current Use: Commercial

DEERING JUNCTION
Building Type: Section Tool House
Railroad: Maine Central
Current Use: Railroad

INDIA STREET
Building Type: Office Building
Railroad: Grand Trunk
Date of Construction: 1902
Current Use: Commercial

ST. JOHN STREET
Building Type: Yard Tower
Railroad: Maine Central
Current Use: Commercial

Building Type: Office Building
Railroad: Maine Central
Date of Construction: 1889, 1898, 1902, 1916
Architect: Bradlee, Winslow & Wetherill of Boston
Current Use: Commercial

THOMPSON'S POINT
Building Type: Office
Railroad: Maine Central
Date of Construction: 1896
Current Use: Commercial

Building Type: Planing Mill
Railroad: Maine Central
Date of Construction: 1911
Current Use: Commercial

Building Type: Car Repair Shop (east end)
Railroad: Maine Central
Date of Construction: 1911
Current Use: Commercial

Building Type: Machine Shop
Railroad: Maine Central
Date of Construction: 1906
Current Use: Commercial

RICHMOND
Building Type: Freight House
Railroad: Maine Central
Date of Construction: 1860
Current Use: Religious

ROCKLAND
Building Type: Engine House (radial)
Railroad: Maine Central
Date of Construction: 1921
Current Use: Railroad

Building Type: Turntable
Railroad: Maine Central
Date of Construction: 1921
Current Use: Railroad

RUMFORD
Building Type: Section Tool House
Railroad: Maine Central
Date of Construction: 1901
Current Use: Railroad

Building Type: Engine House (radial)
Railroad: Maine Central
Date of Construction: 1892
Current Use: Railroad

Building Type: Turntable (air driven)
Railroad: Maine Central
Current Use: Railroad

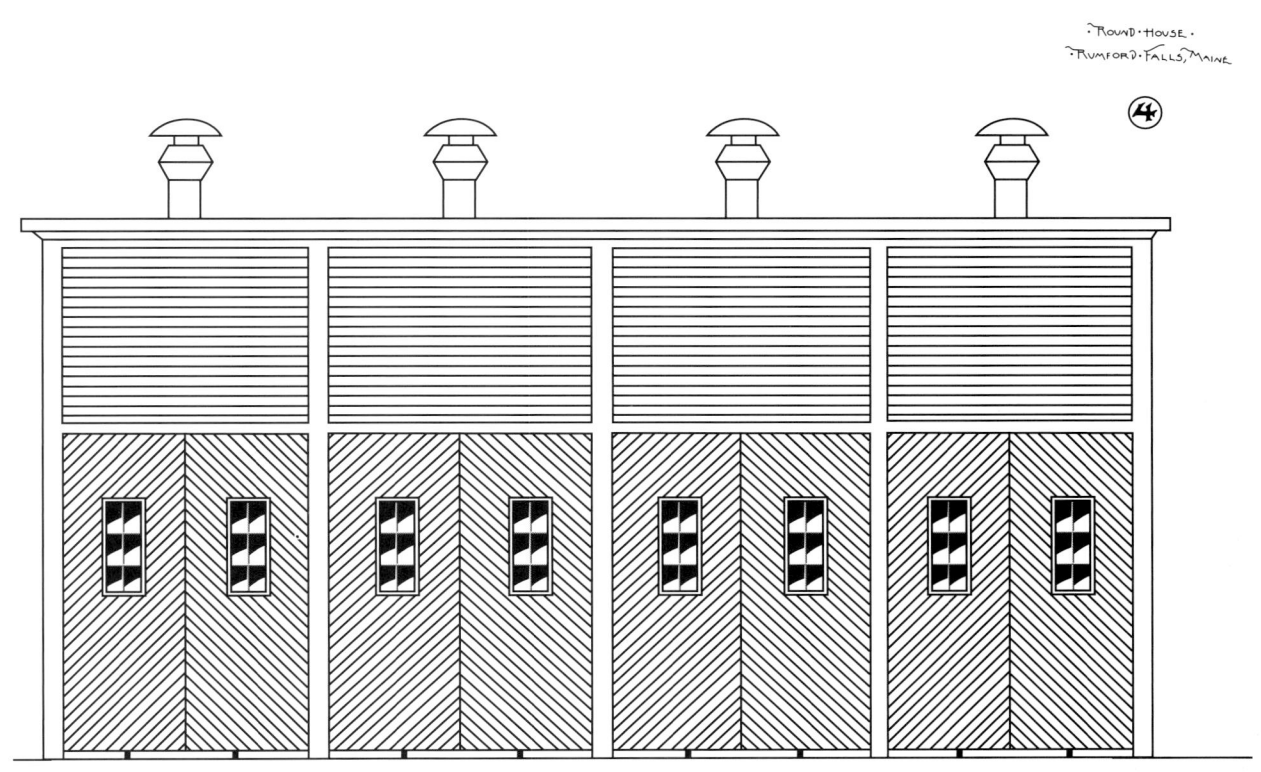

Front Elevation drawing by E. E. Lewis for a Round House [Portland & Rumford Falls Railway], Rumford Falls, Maine, January, 1892

SAINT FRANCIS
Building Type: Turntable (manual)
Railroad: Bangor & Aroostook
Date of Construction: c.1909
Current Use: Not in use

SANFORD
Building Type: Freight House
Railroad: Boston & Maine
Date of Construction: 1903
Current Use: Commercial

SHERMAN
Building Type: Freight House
Railroad: Bangor & Aroostook
Date of Construction: 1903
Current Use: Not in use

SMYRNA (MILLS)
Building Type: Freight House
Railroad: Bangor & Aroostook
Date of Construction: 1902
Current Use: Not in use

SOUTH BERWICK (CONWAY JUNCTION)
Building Type: Turntable Pit
Railroad: Great Falls & South Berwick
Date of Construction: c.1855
Current Use: Preserved site

SOUTH PORTLAND
Building Type: Engine House (radial)
Railroad: Boston & Maine
Current Use: Railroad

Building Type: Turntable
Railroad: Boston & Maine
Current Use: Railroad

STANDISH
Building Type: Turntable Pit
Railroad: Portland & Ogdensburg
Current Use: Not in use

A CATALOGUE OF RAILROAD BUILDINGS

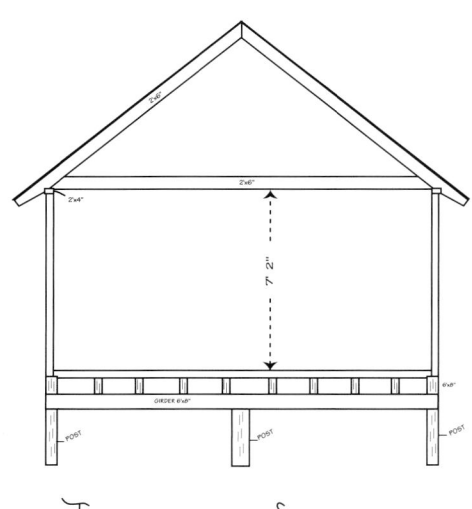

Transverse Section and End Elevation drawings for a Tool House, Portland & Rumford Falls Railway, March, 1894

STOCKHOLM
Building Type: Dwelling House
Railroad: Bangor & Aroostook
Date of Construction: 1905, 1910
Current Use: Residential

Building Type: Freight House
Railroad: Bangor & Aroostook
Date of Construction: 1905
Current Use: Not in use

STRONG
Building Type: Engine House
Railroad: Sandy River
Date of Construction: 1884
Current Use: Commercial

T2R8 NWP (WOODARD)
Building Type: Section Tool House
Railroad: Canadian Pacific
Date of Construction: 1904
Current Use: Railroad

THE FORKS (LAKE MOXIE)
Building Type: Dwelling House
Railroad: Somerset Railway
Current Use: Private Residence

THORNDIKE
Building Type: Section Tool House
Railroad: Belfast & Moosehead Lake
Date of Construction: 1896
Current Use: Railroad

UNITY
Building Type: Turntable (manual)
Railroad: Bangor & Aroostook
Current Use: Railroad (moved from Limestone)

VANBUREN
Building Type: Freight House
Railroad: Bangor & Aroostook
Date of Construction: 1900
Current Use: Not in use

VANCEBORO
Building Type: Section Tool House
Railroad: Maine Central
Date of Construction: 1896
Current Use: Not in use

Building Type: Turntable (electric)
Railroad: Maine Central
Date of Construction: 1912
Current Use: Not in use

CHAPTER IV

WATERVILLE
Building Type: Car Repair Shop
Railroad: Maine Central
Date of Construction: 1886
Current Use: Railroad

Building Type: Transfer Table
Railroad: Maine Central
Current Use: Railroad

Building Type: Engine House (radial)
Railroad: Maine Central
Date of Construction: 1910
Current Use: Railroad

Building Type: Turntable
Railroad: Maine Central
Current Use: Railroad

Building Type: Yard Tower
Railroad: Maine Central
Current Use: Railroad

WELLS (BEACH)
Building Type: Freight House
Railroad: Boston & Maine
Date of Construction: 1884
Current Use: Commercial

WESTBROOK (CUMBERLAND MILLS)
Building Type: Freight House
Railroad: Maine Central
Date of Construction: 1911
Current Use: Commercial

WINTERPORT
Building Type: Coal House
Railroad: Bangor & Aroostook
Current Use: Not in use

Building Type: Section Tool House
Railroad: Bangor & Aroostook
Current Use: Not in use

WISCASSET
Building Type: Section Tool House
Railroad: Wiscasset & Quebec
Date of Construction: 1915
Current Use: Residential (moved from Alna [Sheepscot])

WOODLAND
Building Type: Section Tool House
Railroad: Maine Central
Date of Construction: 1905
Current Use: Railroad

Building Type: Freight House
Railroad: Maine Central
Date of Construction: 1905
Current Use: Railroad

YARMOUTH
Building Type: Freight House
Railroad: Grand Trunk
Date of Construction: 1905
Current Use: Commercial

YARMOUTH (JUNCTION)
Building Type: Freight House
Railroad: Grand Trunk
Current Use: Commercial (Moved from Bethel)

Co. "A" at the Maine Central Railroad Station, Dexter, 1917

BIBLIOGRAPHY

All Aboard for Yesterday: A Nostalgic History of Railroading in Maine. Camden, ME: Down East, 1979.

Amsden, Perham Littlefield. "A History of the Belfast and Moosehead Lake Railroad." Thesis (M.A.). University of Maine, 1951.

Angier, Jerry. *Bangor and Aroostook, The Maine Railroad.* Littleton, MA: Flying Yankee Enterprises, 1986.

Barney, Peter S. The Kennebec Central and Monson Railroads. Kennesaw, GA: A & M Publishing, 1986.

———. *The Bridgton and Saco River: A Technical and Pictorial Review.* Kennesaw, GA: A & M Publishing, 1987.

———. *Structures of the Maine Two-Footers.* Kennesaw, GA: A & M Publishing, 1988.

———. *Handcars, Railcars, and Railbuses of the Sandy River & Rangeley Lakes Railroad.* Kennesaw, GA: A & M Publishing, 1990.

Berg, Walter G., C.E. *Buildings and Structures of American Railroads. A Reference Book for Railroad Managers, Superintendents, Master Mechanics, Engineers, Architects, and Students.* New York: John Wiley & Sons, 1911.

Cardin, Bob. *Old Veazie Railroad, 1836: One of America's Very First Railroads.* Bangor, ME: Cole Land Transportation Museum, 1992.

Chase, Edward E. *Maine Railroads: A History of the Development of the Maine Railroad System.* Portland, ME: A. J. Houston, 1926.

Cornwall, L. Peter, Farrell, Jack. *Ride the Sandy River: A Trip Into the Past on What Was America's Largest Two-Foot Gauge Railroad.* Edmonds, WA: Pacific Fast Mail, 1973.

Crittenden, H. Temple. *The Maine Scenic Route: A History of the Sandy River & Rangeley Lakes Railroad.* Parsons, WVA: McClain Printing Company, 1966.

Drummond, Josiah H. *The Maine Central Railroad System: An Uncompleted Historical Sketch.* [S.1.: s.n.], 1902.

Durnin, Richard G. *Sumner and the Railroad: Buckfield Branch Railroad, Portland & Oxford Central Railroad, Rumford Falls & Buckfield Railroad, Portland & Rumford Falls Railway, Maine Central Railroad.* Norway Center, ME ?: R. G. Durnin, 1998.

European and North American Railway Company. *Memorial of the European and North American Railway Company of Maine.* s.n., 1865.

Freidel, Frederick W. *The Washington County Railway, 1832-1883 and Early Travel in Downeast Maine.* Chatham, NY: Driftwood Press, 1974.

Gallison, Elda. "The Short Route to Europe: A History of the European and North American Railroad." Thesis (M.A.). University of Maine, 1950.

Granger, Alfred, "Designing and Planning of Small Railroad Stations," *Brickbuilder*, Part I, July, 1900 and Part II, October, 1900.

Harlow, Alvin F. *Steelways of New England.* New York: Creative Age Press, Inc., 1946.

Hastings, Philip R. *Philip Ross Hastings: the Boston & Maine, a Photographic Essay.* Locomotive & Railway Preservation [s.l.], 1989.

Hesseltine, Charles D. *Maine Steam Railroad History.* South Portland, ME: The Author, 1968.

_____. *Aroostook Valley Railroad: History of the Potato land Interurban in Northern Maine.* Westbrook, ME: Robertson Books, 1987.

Holt, Jeff. *The Grand Trunk in New England.* Toronto: Railfare Enterprises, Ltd., 1986.

Hutchinson, Doug. *The Rumford Falls and Rangeley Lakes Railroad.* Dixfield, ME: Partridge Lane Publications, 1989.

Johnson, Ron. *Bangor & Aroostook Railroad: From Potatoes to Pulp and Paper.* Portland, ME: Portland Litho., 1983.

_____. *The Best of Maine Railroads.* South Portland, ME ?: s.n., 1985.

Jones, Robert C. *Two Feet Between the Rails: SR&RL,* Volumes I and II, Sundance Books, 1980.

_____. *Two Feet to the Lakes: the Bridgton & Saco River Railroad.* Edmonds, WA: Pacific Fast Mail, 1993.

_____. *Two Feet to the Quarries: the Monson Railroad.* Burlington, VT: Evergreen Press, 1998.

_____. *Two Feet to Togus: the Kennebec Central Railroad.* Burlington, VT: Evergreen Press, 1999.

Jones, Robert and David Register. *Two Feet to Tidewater: WW&F.* 1987.

Kohler, Gary. *Maine Two Foot Pictorial: SR & RL Freight Cars.* Canton, OH: Railroad Publications, 1986.

Lord, Robert F. *Downeast Depots: Maine Railroads in the Steam Era.* Canton, CT: Promotion Productions, 1986.

Marson, Donald G. *Railroads of the Pine Tree State. Vol. I.* La Mirada, CA: Four Ways West Publications, 1999.

MacDougall, Walter Marshall. *The Old Somerset Railroad.* Camden, ME: Down East Books, 2000.

Marcigliano, John. *All Aboard for Union Station.* Unknown, printed by Pilot Press, 1991.

McLin, William Hellen. "The Twenty-Four-Inch Gauge Railroad at Bridgton, Maine: The Life Cycle of a Unit of Transportation." Thesis (M. Ed.). Rhode Island College of Education, 1949.

Mead, Edgar T., Jr. *"Busted and Still Running": The Famous Two-Foot Gauge Railroad of Bridgton, Maine.* Brattleboro, VT: Stephen Greene Press, 1968.

BIBLIOGRAPHY

Mead, Edgar T. *Stories from the Two Foot Gauge: Lilliput Trains in Maine, Wales, and Elsewhere.* Warner, NH?:, 1993.

Meet the Maine Central: The Pine Tree Route, 1960-1981. Portland, ME: 470 Railroad Club, 1981.

Moody, Linwood W. *The Maine Two-Footers: The Story of the Two-Foot Gauge Railroads of Maine.* Berkeley, CA: Howell-North, 1959.

Meeks, Carroll L. V. *The Railroad Station: An Architectural History.* New Haven, CT: Yale University Press, 1956.

Peters, Bradley L. *Maine Central Railroad Company: A Story of Success and Independence.* Portland, ME: Maine Central Railroad Company, 1976.

Pillsbury, David B. "The History of the Atlantic & St. Lawrence Railroad Company." Thesis (M.A.). University of Maine at Orono, 1979.

Poor, Henry Varnum. *History of the Railroads and Canals of the United States.* New York: J. H. Schultz, 1860.

Potter, Janet Greenstein. *Great American Railroad Stations.* New York: John Wiley & Sons, Inc., 1996.

Quebec and Wiscasset Railroad. Quebec, Quebec: s.n., 1889.

Rivard, Paul E. *Lion: The History of an 1846 Locomotive Engine in Maine.* Augusta, ME: Maine State Museum and Machiasport Historical Society, 1987.

Sanborn, Gordon. *Building Maine's Railroads.* (Audiovisual.) Orono, ME: History Media Center, University of Maine at Orono, 1976.

Sheehy, Michael James. "John Alfred Poor and International Railroads: The Early Years to 1860." Thesis (M.A.). University of Maine at Orono, 1974.

Sprague, Richard W. *The Bangor and Aroostook Railroad the First 100 Years, 1891-1991.* (Audiovisual.) Bronson Communications, Inc.: [S.1.], 1991.

Stenberg, Henry G. "A Study of Maine Central Railroad Passenger Service Since 1900." Thesis (M.A.). University of Maine, 1965.

Stilgoe, John R. *Metropolitan Corridor: Railroads and the American Scene.* New Haven, CT: Yale University Press, 1983.

Sullivan, Charles H. *Historical Data Relating to the Machiasport Rail Road.* Whitneyville, ME: C. H. Sullivan, 1940.

The Bangor and Aroostook, 1891-1966. Bangor, ME?: Bangor and Aroostook Railroad Company, 1966.

The Mill's Railroads - Broad and Narrow. Westbrook, ME: S. D. Warren Company, 1974.

The Railroad Lebanon, Maine in Retrospect. Lebanon, ME: Lebanon Historical Society, Wilson Printers, 1992.

Thurlow, Clinton. *The WW&F Two Footer, Hail and Farewell.* Weeks Mills, ME: C. F. Thurlow, 1964.

———. *The Weeks Mills "Y" of the Two-Footer.* Weeks Mills, ME: C. F. Thurlow, c.1964.

———. *Over the Rails by Steam: A Railroad Scrapbook.* Weeks Mills, ME: C. F. Thurlow, 1965.

White, John W. *Early Transportation in Northernmost New England, 1820-1870.* New England Association of Social Studies Teachers [s.l.], 1955.

White, John William. "The Bangor and Aroostook Railroad, The County It Serves and The People Who Built It." Thesis (M.A.). University of Maine, 1952.

Whitney, Deane Spurling. "A History of the Maine Shore Line Railroad." Thesis (M.A.). University of Maine, 1961.

Whitney, Roger A. *The Monson Railroad.* Westbrook, ME: Robertson Books, 1989.

Wiggin, Ruby Crosby. *Albion on the Narrow Gauge.* Clinton, ME ?: s.n., 1964.

———. *Big Dreams and Little Wheels.* Clinton, ME: s.n., 1971.

Zimmerman, Michael W. *The Sunrise Route: A History of the Railroads of Washington County, Maine.* Brewer, ME: Cay-Bel Publishing Company, 1985.

BIBLIOGRAPHY

View from track side of the Grand Trunk Railway Station, Portland, 1905

View of the Belfast & Moosehead Lake Railroad Station, Belfast, c. 1910

APPENDIX A

Development Era of Maine Railroads
1832 – 1932 CHRONOLOGY

In the century between 1832 and 1932, hundreds of companies were chartered by the Maine Legislature or were organized under State law for the purpose of building railroads between specific geographic points. The following chronology contains information about many of those railroad companies, including the year in which they were chartered or organized, the date in which track segments were opened, and subsequent actions that effected the company organization. It is not, however, an exhaustive list of all the companies which were chartered or incorporated to construct railroads. Instead, it focuses on railroads that were ultimately built, regardless of whether the particular corridor was developed shortly after a charter was initially granted or whether it took years and a successor company to realize the project.

The format of the chronology is organized with the charter and construction dates in the left hand column, the name of the company and respective dates of significance in the center column, and the location of associated track segments in the right hand column.

Many primary and secondary sources have been consulted in the development of this chronology including government and corporate records. Of particular value was H. Walter Leavitt's "Chronology of Maine Railroads," which was appended to his paper titled *Some Interesting Phases of the Development of Transportation in Maine*, and published in 1940 by the Maine Technology Experiment Station. Every effort has been made to insure that the information presented here is accurate, but no claim is made that it is a definitive chronology.

Finally, a word is in order about the use of the term "Charter." Until 1876, it appears that the Legislature reserved the sole right to authorize — or charter — railroad companies. With the passage of the general railroad law of 1876, the Legislature empowered the railroad commissioners to approve the organization of railroad companies without requiring that they be legislatively chartered (although the practice continued nonetheless). For the purposes of this chronology, however, the term "Charter" may refer to either the legislative action, the action of incorporation or the organizational approval by the railroad commissioners.

Key to Abbreviations:

* – railroad not built
acq – acquired
B – date track opened
BG – Broad Gauge (more than 4' 8 1/2" between rails)
C – charter, organization or incorporation date
nc – name change
NG – Narrow Gauge (less than 4' 8 1/2" between rails)
reorg – reorganized
RR – railroad
RY – railway
SG – Standard Gauge (4' 8 1/2" between rails)

C - 1832 * Bangor & Oldtown RY Co.

C - 1832 * Calais RY Co.
    1838 (nc) **Calais RR Co.**
      (horse)
B - 1839   Calais - Salmon Falls
    1849 (acq by) Calais & Baring RR

C - 1832 * Old Town RY
    1833 (C acq by) Bangor & Piscataquis Canal

C - 1833 **Bangor & Piscataquis Canal & RR Co.** (B&PC)
B - 1836   Bangor - Old Town
B - 1854   Old Town - Milford
    1855 (nc) **Bangor, Old Town & Milford RR**
    1871 (acq by) European & North American RY Co.

C - 1836 * Belfast & Bangor RR

APPENDIX A

C - 1836   * Belfast & Gardiner RR

C - 1836   * Belfast & Quebec RR Corp.

C - 1836   **Eastern RR of Massachusetts** (ER)
- 1842   (lease) Portland, Saco & Portsmouth
- 1880   (operator) Old Orchard Junction
- 1884   (lease to) Boston & Maine
- 1887   (acq by) Boston & Maine

C - 1836   **Kennebec & Portland RR Co.** (K&P)
- B - 1849   Yarmouth - Bath
- B - 1850   Yarmouth - South Portland
- B - 1851   Brunswick - Augusta
- 1862   (acq by) Portland & Kennebec

C - 1836   **Maine, New Hampshire & Massachusetts RR Corp.**
- 1841   (nc) **Boston & Maine RR Co.** (B&M)
- 1842   (operator) Great Falls & South Berwick Branch
- B - 1873   South Berwick - Portland
- 1880   (operator) Orchard Beach
- 1883   (lease of) Kennebunk & Kennebunkport
- 1884   (lease of) Eastern / Maine Central
- 1887   (acq) Orchard Beach
- 1887   (acq) Portland & Rochester
- 1887   (acq) Portland, Saco & Portsmouth
- 1897   (operator) York Harbor & Beach

C - 1837   * Calais & Baring RY

C - 1837   **Portland, Saco & Portsmouth RR Co.** (PS&P)
- B - 1842   Portland - Portsmouth
- 1842   (lease to) Eastern / Boston & Maine
- 1871   (lease to) Eastern
- 1884   Eastern / PS&P (lease to) Boston & Maine
- 1887   (acq by) Boston & Maine

C - 1839	* Calais & Baring RR (former C&BRY)	
C - 1841	**Great Falls & Conway RR Co.** (GF&C)	
B - 1849		New Hampshire - Lebanon
		New Hampshire
C - 1841	**Great Falls & South Berwick Branch RR Co.** (GF&SB)	
B - 1842		New Hampshire - South Berwick
	1842 (operated by) Boston & Maine	
C - 1842	**Palmer & Machiasport RR Corp.** (P&M)	
B - 1842		Machiasport - Whitneyville
	1845 (nc) **Machiasport RR**	
	1892 (discontinued)	
C - 1845	**Androscoggin & Kennebec RR** (A&K) (BG 5'6")	
B - 1848		Danville Junction - Lewiston
B - 1849		Lewiston - Waterville
	1862 (consolidated as) Maine Central	
C - 1845	**Atlantic & St. Lawrence RR** (A&SL) (BG 5'6")	
B - 1848		Portland - Danville Junction
B - 1850		Portland Waterfront
B - 1851		Danville Junction - Gilead
B - 1853		Gilead - Montreal
	1855 (lease to) Grand Trunk	
	1859 (acq by) Grand Trunk	
	1872 (changed to SG)	

APPENDIX A

C - 1845	**Penobscot & Kennebec RR** (PE&K)		
	(BG 5'6")		
B - 1853			Waterville - Fairfield
B - 1854			Fairfield - Pittsfield
B - 1855			Pittsfield - Bangor
	1856	(lease to) Androscoggin & Kennebec	
	1862	(consolidated as) Maine Central	

C - 1846	**York & Cumberland RR Co.** (Y&C)		
B - 1850			Portland - Saco River
	1865	(acq by) Portland & Rochester	

C - 1847	**Buckfield Branch RR Co.** (BB)		
	(BG 5'6")		
B - 1850			Mechanic Falls - Buckfield
B - 1855			Buckfield - East Sumner
	1857	(acq by) Portland & Oxford Central	

C - 1847	* Franklin & Kennebec RR Co.

C - 1847	**Moosehead Lake RY** (ML)	
	(NG 3'6"+/-) (oxen)	
B - 1847		Moosehead Lake - West Branch Penobscot

C - 1847	* Penobscot RR	
	1863 (C acq by) European & North American	

C - 1848	**Androscoggin RR Co.** (AN)		
	(BG 5'6")		
B - 1852			Leeds Junction - Livermore Falls
B - 1859			Livermore Falls - West Farmington
B - 1861	(changed to SG)		Leeds - Brunswick
B - 1861			Crowley's Junction - Lewiston
	1865	(operated by) Leeds & Farmington	
	1871	(lease to) Maine Central	
	1911	(acq by) Maine Central	

C - 1848	* Belfast & Waterville RR Co.	
C - 1848	**Somerset & Kennebec RR** (S&K)	
B - 1853		Augusta - Waterville
B - 1855		Waterville - Fairfield
B - 1856		Fairfield - Skowhegan
	1856 (lease to) Kennebec & Portland	
	1864 (lease to) Portland & Kennebec	
	1870 (lease to) Maine Central	
	1874 (acq by) Maine Central	
C - 1849	**Calais & Baring RR** (C&B)	
	(former CRR) (horse to steam)	
B - 1852		Salmon Falls - Baring
	1870 (nc) **St. Croix & Penobscot RR**	
	1870 (acq) Lewy's Island	
	1899 (acq by) Washington County	
C - 1849	Penobscot & Kennebec RR Co.	
	1849 (nc) Penobscot, Lincoln & Kennebec RR Co. (PL&K)	
	1864 (nc) **Knox & Lincoln RR Co.** (K&L)	
B - 1871		Woolwich - Rockland, Kennebec Ferry
B - 1876		Rockland
	1883 (acq by) Penobscot Shore Line RR Co.	
C - 1850	**European & North American RY Co.** (E&NA)	
	(BG 5'6")	
	1863 (acq C) Penobscot	
B - 1868		Bangor - Olamon
B - 1869		Olamon - Mattawamkeag
	1869 (acq) Bangor, Old Town & Milford	
B - 1871		Mattawamkeag - Vanceboro
B - 1870	European & North American of N.B.	Vanceboro - St. John, N.B.
	1877 (changed to SG)	
	1880 (reorg) European & North American	
	1882 (lease to) Maine Central	
B - 1887		Enfield - West Enfield

	1890	Canadian Pacific / Maine Central	
		(joint use Mattawamkeag-Vanceboro)	
B - 1891			West Enfield - Howland
	1955	(acq by) Maine Central	

C - 1853	**Belfast & Moosehead Lake RR Co.** (B&ML)
B - 1870	Belfast - Burnham Junction
	1871 (lease to) Maine Central
	1926 (control to) City of Belfast

C - 1853 **Dexter & Newport RR** (D&N)
(BG 5'6")

B - 1868   Newport - Dexter
    1869 (lease to) Maine Central
    1871 (changed to SG)
    1897 (lease renew) Maine Central
    1939 (acq by) Maine Central

C - 1853 **Grand Trunk RY of Canada** (GTR)
    1853 (lease of) A&SL
    1859 (acq) A&SL
    1872 (changed to SG)
    1874 (lease of) Lewiston & Auburn
    1880 (lease of) Norway Branch
    1920 (acq by) Canadian National

C - 1854 * Aroostook RR

C - 1854 * Kennebec & Wiscasset RR Co.
    1862 charter revived
    1873 (nc) Wiscasset & Moosehead Lake RR

C - 1854 **Lewy's Island RR Co.** (LI)
B - 1856   Baring - New Brunswick Border
B - 1857   New Brunswick Border - Princeton
    1870 (acq by) St Croix & Penobscot

C - 1854		Wiscasset & Quebec RR (W&Q)	
	1876	(nc) **Wiscasset & Quebec RR Co.** (W&Q)	
		(NG 2'0")	
B - 1895			Wiscasset - Albion
B - 1897			Albion - Burnham
	1899	(trustees)	
	1890	(reorg) Wiscasset & Quebec RR	
	1901	(acq by) Wiscasset, Waterville & Farmington	

C - 1856		**Maine Central RR** (MEC)	
		(BG 5'6")	
	1862	(consolidated) Androscoggin & Kennebec	
	1862	(consolidated) Penobscot & Kennebec	
	1869	(lease of) Dexter & Newport	
	1870	(lease of) Portland & Kennebec	
	1870	(lease of) Somerset & Kennebec	
B - 1870			North Yarmouth - Royal Junction
	1871	(changed to SG) A&K / PE&K	
B - 1871			Danville Junction - Cumberland Junction
	1871	(lease of) Androscoggin	
	1871	(lease of) Leeds & Farmington	
	1871	(lease of) Belfast & Moosehead Lake	
	1873	(control by) Eastern	
	1874	(acq) Portland & Kennebec	
	1874	(acq) Somerset & Kennebec	
	1874	(acq) Leeds & Farmington	
	1882	(lease of) European & North American	
	1883	(lease of) Eastern Maine	
	1884	(lease of) Maine Shore Line	
	1884	Eastern / Maine Central	
		(lease to) Boston & Maine	
B - 1884			Bar Harbor Ferry
	1887	(lease) Dexter & Piscataquis	
	1887	(acq) Maine Shore Line	
	1887	(lease of) Portland & Ogdensburg	

APPENDIX A

	1890 Maine Central / Canadian Pacific (Mattawamkeag-Vanceboro contract use)	
	1891 (lease of) Knox & Lincoln (Penobscot Shore Line)	
	1901 (acq) Knox & Lincoln (Penobscot Shore Line)	
	1904 (control of) Washington County	
	1907 (lease of) Portland & Rumford Falls	
	1907 (control of) Somerset	
	1907 (acq) Rumford Falls & Rangeley Lakes	
	1910 (lease) Sebasticook & Moosehead	
	1911 (acq) Androscoggin	
	1911 (acq) Sandy River & Rangeley Lakes	
	1911 (acq) Sebasticook & Moosehead	
	1911 (acq) Somerset	
	1911 (acq) Washington County	
B - 1912		Mainstream - Harmony
	1912 (acq) Bridgton & Saco River	
	1914 (acq) Rangeley Lakes & Megantic	
	1914 (regain control from) Boston & Maine / NY, NH & H	
	1926 (end lease of) Belfast & Moosehead Lake	
B - 1927		Bath Bridge
	1935 (acq) Eastern Maine	
	1939 (acq) Dexter & Newport	
	1939 (acq) Dexter & Piscataquis	
	1943 (acq) Portland & Ogdensburg	
	1946 (acq) Portland & Rumford Falls	
	1955 (acq) European & North American	

C - 1857	**Portland & Oxford Central RR Co.** (P&OC) (former BB) (BG 5'6")	
B - 1867		East Sumner - Hartford
B - 1870		Hartford - Canton
	1872 (changed to SG)	
	1874 (acq by) Rumford Falls & Buckfield	

C - 1860	**Somerset RR Co.** (SRR)	
B - 1873		Oakland - Norridgewock
B - 1874		Norridgewock - Madison
B - 1875		Madison - North Anson
	1883 (acq by) Somerset RY	

C - 1861	**Bangor & Piscataguis RR** (B&P)	
	(BG 5'6")	
B - 1869		Old Town - Dover
	1874 (lease to) European & North American	
B - 1871		Dover - Guilford
	1877 (changed to SG)	
B - 1878		Guilford - Blanchard
B - 1884		Blanchard - Greenville
	1892 (lease to) Bangor & Aroostook	
	1899 (acq by) Bangor & Aroostook	

C - 1862	**Portland & Kennebec RR** (PO&K)
	(former K&P)
	1864 (lease of) Somerset & Kennebec
	1870 (lease to) Maine Central
	1874 (acq by) Maine Central

C - 1864	**Limerock RR Co.** (LR)	
B - 1888		Rockland
	1942 (discontinued)	

C - 1865	**Leeds & Farmington RR Co.** (L&F)	
	1865 (operator) Androscoggin	
B - 1870		West Farmington - Farmington
	1871 (lease to) Maine Central	
	1874 (acq by) Maine Central	

APPENDIX A

C - 1866	**Portland & Rochester RR Co.** (P&RO)	
	1865 (acq) York & Cumberland	
B - 1870		Saco River - Springvale
B - 1872		Springvale - Rochester, N.H.
	1900 (acq by) Boston & Maine	

C - 1867	**Houlton Branch RR Co.** (HB)	
B - 1870		New Brunswick - Houlton
	1882 (leased by) New Brunswick	
	1890 (NBRY leased by) Canadian Pacific	

C - 1867	**Portland & Ogdensburg RR Co.** (P&O)	
B - 1870		Portland - West Baldwin
B - 1871		West Baldwin - North Conway
	1886 (acq by) Portland & Ogdensburg RY	

C - 1868	* Penobscot Bay & River RR Co.

C - 1868	* Portland & Rutland RR Co.
	1870 (nc) Portland, Rutland, Oswego & Chicago RY

C - 1870	Penobscot & Union River RR Co. (P&UR)	
	1873 (nc) **Bucksport & Bangor RR Co.** (B&B)	
	(BG 5'6")	
B - 1874		Bucksport - Bangor
	1877 (lease to) European & North American	
	1877 (changed to NG 3'0")	
	1882 (acq by) Eastern Maine	

C - 1871	**Old Orchard Junction RR Co.** (OOJ)	
B - 1880		Old Orchard Beach
	1880 (operated by) Eastern	

C - 1871	* Penobscot & Lake Megantic RR Co.
	1885 (C acq by) International Railway of Maine

C - 1872	**Lewiston & Auburn RR Co.** (L&A)	
B - 1874		Auburn - Lewiston
	1874 (leased by) Grand Trunk	

C - 1872	**Norway Branch RR** (NB)	
B - 1879		South Paris - Norway
	1880 (leased by) Grand Trunk	

C - 1873	**Aroostook River RR** (AR)	
	(NG 3'0")	
B - 1876		New Brunswick - Caribou
B - 1881		Caribou - Presque Isle
	1882 (leased by) New Brunswick	
	1890 (NBRY leased by) Canadian Pacific	

C - 1874	* Messalonskee & Kennebec RR Co.

C - 1874	**Rumford Falls & Buckfield RR Co.** (RF&B)	
	(former P&OC)	
	1878 (changed to SG)	
B - 1879		Canton - Gilbertville
	1890 (lease to) Portland & Rumford Falls	

C - 1876	**Orchard Beach RR Co.** (OB)	
B - 1880		Old Orchard Beach-Camp Ellis
	1880 (operated by) Boston & Maine	
	1923 (discontinued)	

C - 1879	**Sandy River RR** (SR)	
	(NG 2'0")	
B - 1879		Farmington - Phillips
	1898 (acq) Farmington & Megantic	
	1898 (acq) Kingfield & Dead River	
	1908 (acq by) Sandy River & Rangeley Lakes	

APPENDIX A

C - 1880   * Bridgton & Presumpscot River RR

C - 1881   **Bangor & Katahdin Iron Works RY** (B&KIW)
B - 1881   Milo-Brownville
B - 1882   Brownville - Katahdin Iron Works

     1889   (lease to) Bangor & Piscataquis
     1901   (acq by) Bangor and Aroostook

C - 1881   **Bridgton & Saco River RR Co.** (B&SR)
          (NG 2'0")
B - 1882   Hiram - Bridgton
B - 1898   Bridgton - Harrison

     1912   (acq by) Maine Central
     1927   (receivership)
     1930   (acq by) Bridgton & Harrison

C - 1881   **International RY of Maine** (IRM)
     1881   (operated by) **Canadian Pacific RY Co.**
     1885   (acq C) Penobscot & Lake Megantic
     1886   (C acq by) Atlantic & Northwest RY
     1888   (lease to) Canadian Pacific
B - 1889   Lake Megantic - Mattawamkeag

C - 1881   **Maine Shore Line RR Co.** (MSL)
B - 1884   Brewer Junction - Mt. Desert Ferry

     1884   (lease to) Maine Central
     1887   (acq by) Maine Central

C - 1881   **Monson & Athens RR Co.** (M&A)
          (NG 2'0")
B - 1883   Abbot - Monson
     1885   (nc) **Monson RR**
B - 1909   Monson - Eighteen Quarry
     1943   (discontinued)

C - 1882	**Green Mountain RY** (GM)	
	(NG 4'7 1/2") (cog)	
B - 1883		Cadillac Mountain

C - 1882	**Kennebunk & Kennebunkport RR** (K&K)	
B - 1883		
	1883 (leased to) Boston & Maine	
	1925 (discontinued)	

C - 1883	**Eastern Maine RY Co.** (EMRY)	
	(SG) (former B&B)	
	1883 (lease to) Maine Central	
	1935 (acq by) Maine Central	

C - 1883	**Franklin & Megantic RR** (F&M)	
	(NG 2'0")	
B - 1884		Strong - Kingfield
B - 1886		Mt. Abram Bridge
B - 1894	(subsidiary) **Kingfield & Dead River RR**	Kingfield
		Carrabasset
	1898 (acq by) Franklin & Megantic	
	1898 (receivership) Kingfield & Dead River	
	1898 (control by) Sandy River	

C - 1883	**Somerset RY** (SRY)	
	(former SRR)	
B - 1887		North Anson - Embden
B - 1890		Embden - Bingham
	1904 (nc) **Somerset RY Co.** (SRYC)	
B - 1905		Bingham - Deadwater
B - 1906		Deadwater - Moosehead Lake
		Austin Pond Bridge
	1907 (control by) Maine Central	
	1911 (acq by) Maine Central	

APPENDIX A

C - 1883   **York Harbor & Beach RR Co.** (YH&B)
B - 1887   Kittery - York Beach
          1897   (operator) Boston & Maine
          1927   (discontinued)

C - 1883   * Anson & New Portland RR

C - 1883   * Mount Desert RY

C - 1886   * Atlantic & Northwest RY
          1886   (acq C) International RY of Maine
          1886   (leased to) Canadian Pacific

C - 1886   **Portland & Ogdensburg RY** (P&ORY)
                (former P&ORR)
          1887   (lease to) Maine Central
          1943   (acq by) Maine Central

C - 1886   **Rockport RR** (RR)
                (NG 3'0")
B - 1886   Rockport
          1898   (discontinued)

C - 1886   **Sebasticook & Moosehead RR Co.** (S&M)
B - 1886   Pittsfield - Hartland
B - 1901   Hartland - Mainstream
          1903   Sebasticook & Moosehead (reorg)
          1910   (lease to) Maine Central
          1911   (acq by) Maine Central

C - 1887   **Portland Union Railway Station Co.** (PURS)
          1911   (nc) **Portland Terminal Co.**
          1911   (lease of) Portland, So. Portland, Westbrook
                        property of Boston & Maine / Maine Central

C - 1888	**Dexter & Piscataquis RR** (D&P)		
	1888 (lease to) Maine Central		
B - 1888			Dover - Dexter
	1939 (acq by) Maine Central		

C - 1889	**Georges Valley RR Co.** (GV)		
B - 1893			Warren - Union
	1899 (nc) **Knox RR**		

C - 1889	**Kennebec Central RR Co.** (KC)		
	(NG 2'0")		
B - 1889			Randolph - Chelsea
	1929 (discontinued)		

C - 1889	**Penobscot Shore Line RR Co.** (PSL)		
	1891 (nc) **Knox & Lincoln RY**		
	1891 (lease to) Maine Central		
	1901 (acq by) Maine Central		

C - 1889	**Phillips & Rangeley RR Co.** (P&RA)		
	(NG 2'0")		
B - 1890			Phillips - South Branch Dead River
B - 1891			Dead River - Rangeley
B - 1902			Number Six Bridge
B - 1902	(subsidiary) **Madrid RR**		Brackett's Junction - Littlefield's
	1905 (receivership)		
B - 1906			Mount Abram
	1908 Phillips & Rangeley / Madrid (acq by) Sandy River & Rangeley Lakes		

C - 1890	**Portland & Rumford Falls RY Co.** (P&RFRY)		
	1890 (lease of) Rumford Falls & Buckfield		
B - 1892			Gilbertville - Rumford Falls
B - 1894			Mechanic Falls - Rumford Junction

B - 1896			Canton - Peterson Rips
B - 1897			Peterson Rips - Chisholm
B - 1899			Chisholm - Livermore Falls
	1907	(lease to) Portland & Rumford Falls RR	

....

C - 1891	**Bangor and Aroostook RR** (BAR)		
	Aroostook Construction Co.		
	(formed to build line)		
	1892	(lease of) Bangor & Piscataquis	
	1892	(lease of) Bangor & Katahdin Iron Works	
B - 1894			Brownville - Houlton
B - 1895			Houlton - Caribou - Fort Fairfield
			Ashland Jct. - Ashland
B - 1897			Caribou - Limestone
	189 ?	(acq) Aroostook Northern	
B - 1899			Caribou - Van Buren
	1899	(acq) Bangor & Piscataquis	
	1901	(acq) Bangor & Katahdin Iron Works	
	1901	(lease of) Patten & Sherman	
B - 1902	Fish River RR		Ashland - Fort Kent
	1903	(acq) Fish River	
	1905	(lease of) Northern Maine Seaport	
B - 1907			Packard - South Lagrange
	1907	(acq) Schoodic Stream	
B - 1909	St. John and Washburn extensions		Van Buren - Grand Isle
			Fort Kent - St. Francis
B - 1910			Fort Kent - Grand Isle
			Ashland - Stockholm
			Mapleton - Presque Isle
C - 1913	Van Buren Bridge Co. (subsidiary of BAR)		
B - 1915	Van Buren Bridge Co.		St. John River Bridge
	1919	(acq) Northern Maine Seaport	

....

C - 1893	**Washington County RR Co.** (WCRR)	
B - 1899		Ayers Junction - St. Croix Junction
		Washington Junction - Ayers Junction
		Ayers Junction - Eastport
	1898 (acq) Calais & Baring	
	1899 (acq) St. Croix & Penobscot	
	1899 (acq) Lewy's Island	
	1903 (acq by) Washington County RY	

C - 1894	**Rumford Falls & Rangeley Lakes RR Co.** (RF&RL)	
B - 1895		Rumford Falls - Houghton
		Letter "E," TWP 6 Bridge
B - 1896		Houghton - Bemis
B - 1901		Rangeley Station - Haines Landing
B - 1902		Bemis - Oquossoc
	1907 (lease to) Portland & Rumford Falls	
	1907 (acq by) Maine Central	

C - 1895	* Farmington, Waterville & Wiscasset RR Co.

C - 1895	**Patten & Sherman RR** (P&S)	
B - 1895		Sherman - Patten
	1901 (lease to) Bangor & Aroostook	

C - 1895	**Waterville & Wiscasset RR Co.** (W&W)	
	(NG 2'0")	
	1901 (C acq by) Wiscasset, Waterville & Farmington	
B - 1902		Weeks Mills - Winslow

C - 1897	**Aroostook Northern RR** (ANR)	
B - 1897		Caribou - Limestone

APPENDIX A

C - 1897	**Franklin & Megantic RY** (F&MRY)	
	(Former F&M) (NG 2'0")	
	1898 (acq by) Sandy River	
B - 1900		Carrabasset - Bigelow
B - 1905		Alder Stream Bridge - Hammond Field Bridge
	1908 (acq by) Sandy River & Rangeley Lakes	

C - 1897	* Franklin, Somerset & Kennebec RR Co.
	1901 (C acq by) Wiscasset, Waterville & Farmington

C - 1901	**Wiscasset, Waterville & Farmington RR Co.** (WW&F)
	(NG 2'0")
	1901 (acq) Wiscasset & Quebec
	1901 (acq C) Waterville & Wiscasset
	1901 (acq C) Franklin, Somerset & Kennebec
	1907 (nc) **Wiscasset, Waterville & Farmington RY Co.**
	1925 Discontinued

C - 1902	**Aroostook Valley RR Co.** (AVR)	
	(traction)	
B - 1910		Presque Isle - Washburn
B - 1911		Washburn - Woodland
B - 1912		Woodland - New Sweden
		Woodland - Caribou

C - 1903	**Eustis RR Co.** (EU)	
	(NG 2'0")	
B - 1903		Dallas - Stratton Junction
B - 1905		Dago Bridge
	1908 (leased by) Sandy River & Rangeley Lakes	
	1911 (acq by) Sandy River & Rangeley Lakes	

C - 1903   * Maine Midland RR

C - 1903   **Washington County RY** (WCRY)
- (former WCRR)
- 1904 (control by) Maine Central
- 1911 (acq by) Maine Central

C - 1905   **Northern Maine Seaport RR Co.** (NMS)
B - 1905   South Lagrange - Searsport
                                      Cape Jellison Bridge
- 1905 (lease to) Bangor and Aroostook
- 1919 (acq by) Bangor and Aroostook

C - 1906   **Schoodic Stream RR Co.** (SS)
B - 1907   Millinocket - East Millinocket
- 1907 (acq by) Bangor and Aroostook

C - 1907   **Portland & Rumford Falls RR** (P&RFRR)
- 1907 (lease of) Portland & Rumford Falls RY
- 1907 (lease of) Rumford Falls & Rangeley Lakes
- 1907 (lease to) Maine Central
- 1946 (acq by) Maine Central

C - 1908   **Sandy River & Rangeley Lakes RR** (SL&RL)
- (NG 2'0")
- 1908 (consolidated) Sandy River
- 1908 (consolidated) Franklin & Megantic
- 1908 (consolidated) Kingfield & Dead River
- 1908 (acq) Phillips & Rangeley
- 1908 (acq) Madrid
- 1908 (lease of) Eustis
- 1911 (acq) Eustis
- 1911 (acq by) Maine Central

B - 1912   Perham Bridge
B - 1915   Langtown
- 1923 (receivership)

APPENDIX A

C - 1909	**Rangeley Lakes & Megantic RR Co.** (RL&M)	
B - 1912		West Kamankeag - Kennebago
	1914 (acq by) Maine Central	

C - 1914	**Maine Railways Cos.** (MRC)	
	1914 (control of) Maine Central	

G - 1917	(railroad control by) U.S. Government	
	1920 (railroad control released) U.S. Government	

C - 1927	**Bridgton & Harrison RY Co.** (B&H)	
	(NG 2'0")	
	1930 (acq) Bridgton & Saco River	
	1941 (discontinued)	

LOGGING RAILROADS (not chartered)

B - 1911	**Hollingsworth & Company**	Kineo - Bald Mountain Township
	1922 (discontinued)	

B - 1914	**Bald Mountain RR**	Boundary Bald Mountain vicinity
	1926 (discontinued)	

B - 1926	**Eagle Lake & West Branch RR**	Eagle Lake - Umbazooksus Lake
	1933 (discontinued)	

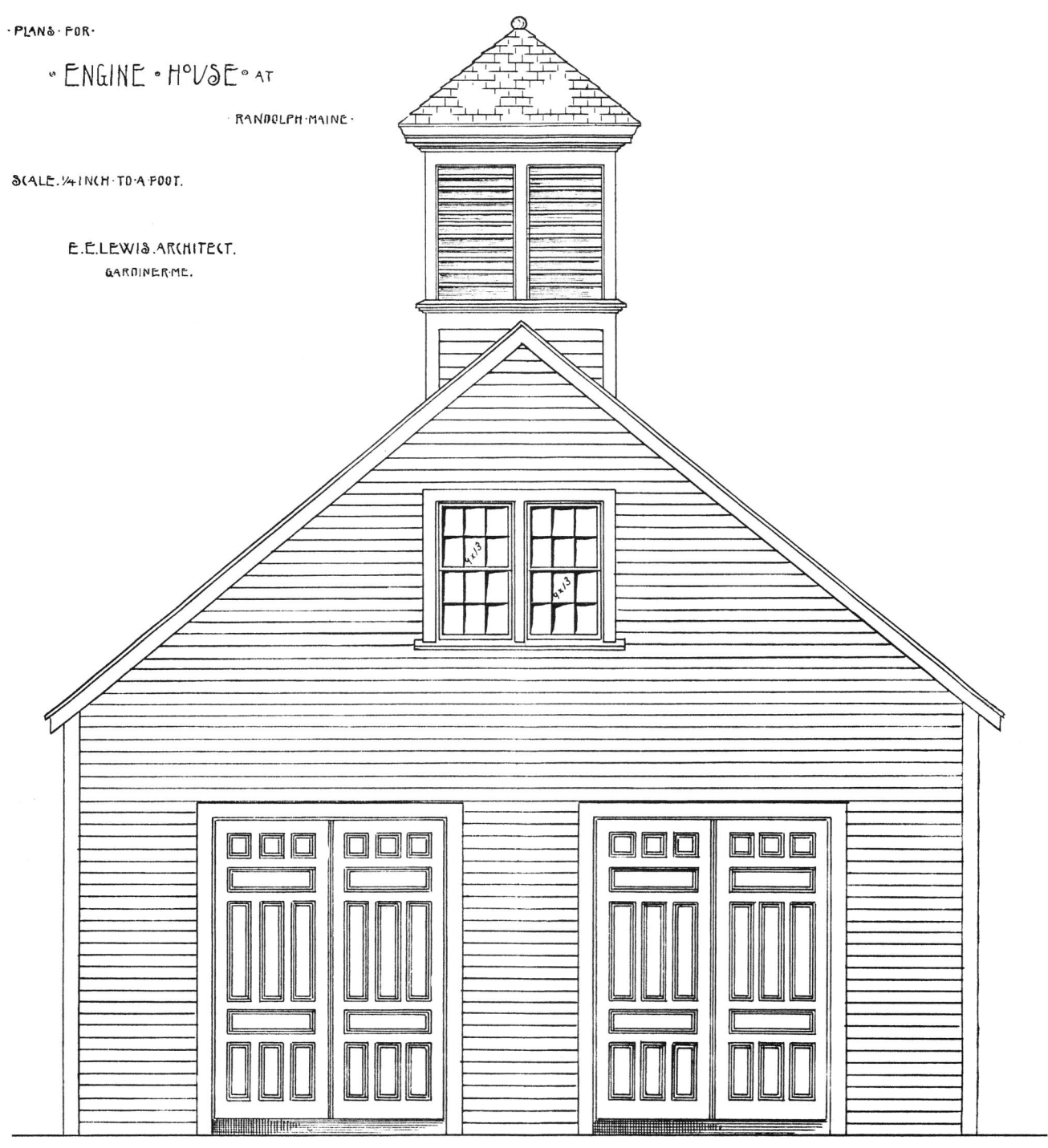

Front Elevation drawing by E. E. Lewis for an Engine House at Randolph, Maine, Kennebec Central Railroad, 1890

APPENDIX B

Railroad Building Drawings

Appendix B is an inventory of railroad building drawings which are located in the collections of the Maine Historic Preservation Commission in Augusta and the Maine Historical Society in Portland, respectively. The drawings are arranged alphabetically by town, with individual entries describing the building type, date, and architect or engineer as indicated on the drawings. Unless otherwise noted, all drawings are for Maine Central Railroad properties.

MAINE HISTORIC PRESERVATION COMMISSION COLLECTION

Augusta
Station by Robert C. Reamer, architect

Belgrade
Station, 1849, Androscoggin & Kennebec Railroad

Benton
Signal House

Bingham
Engine House, 1924

Bowdoinham
Station, 1892

Canton
Gilbertville Combination Station by E. E. Lewis, architect and Frederick Danforth, civil engineer, 1892, Portland & Rumford Falls Railway

Carrabasset
Combination Station, 1898, Kingfield & Dead River Railroad

Chelsea
Togus Station by E. E. Lewis, architect, 1890, Kennebec Central Railroad

Cumberland
Station

Dixfield
Station by E. E. Lewis, architect and Frederick Danforth, civil
   engineer, 1893, Portland & Rumford Falls Railway

Fairfield
Hinckley Station

Fryeburg
Baggage Room

Greenbush
Station by A. Y. Hilton, architect, 1882

Greene
Station, 1849, Androscoggin & Kennebec Railroad

Harmony
Freight House, 1912

Indian Stream Township
Indian Pond Station, Somerset Railway

Leeds
Station, 1849, Androscoggin & Kennebec Railroad

Lewiston
Station, 1890

Machiasport
Station and Residence, 1909, Washington County Railway

Madison
Station by William R. Miller, architect, Somerset Railway

Mechanic Falls
Freight House by Frederick Danforth, civil engineer, 1893,
   Portland & Rumford Falls Railway
Freight Station by Frederick Danforth, civil engineer, 1894,
   Portland & Rumford Falls Railway Station by Frederick Danforth,
   civil engineer, 1894, Portland & Rumford Falls Railway

Monmouth
Station, 1849, Androscoggin & Kennebec Railroad

Moscow
Deadwater Station, 1913

APPENDIX B

Section drawing of the Tank House at Dresden, Maine Central Railroad, c. 1907

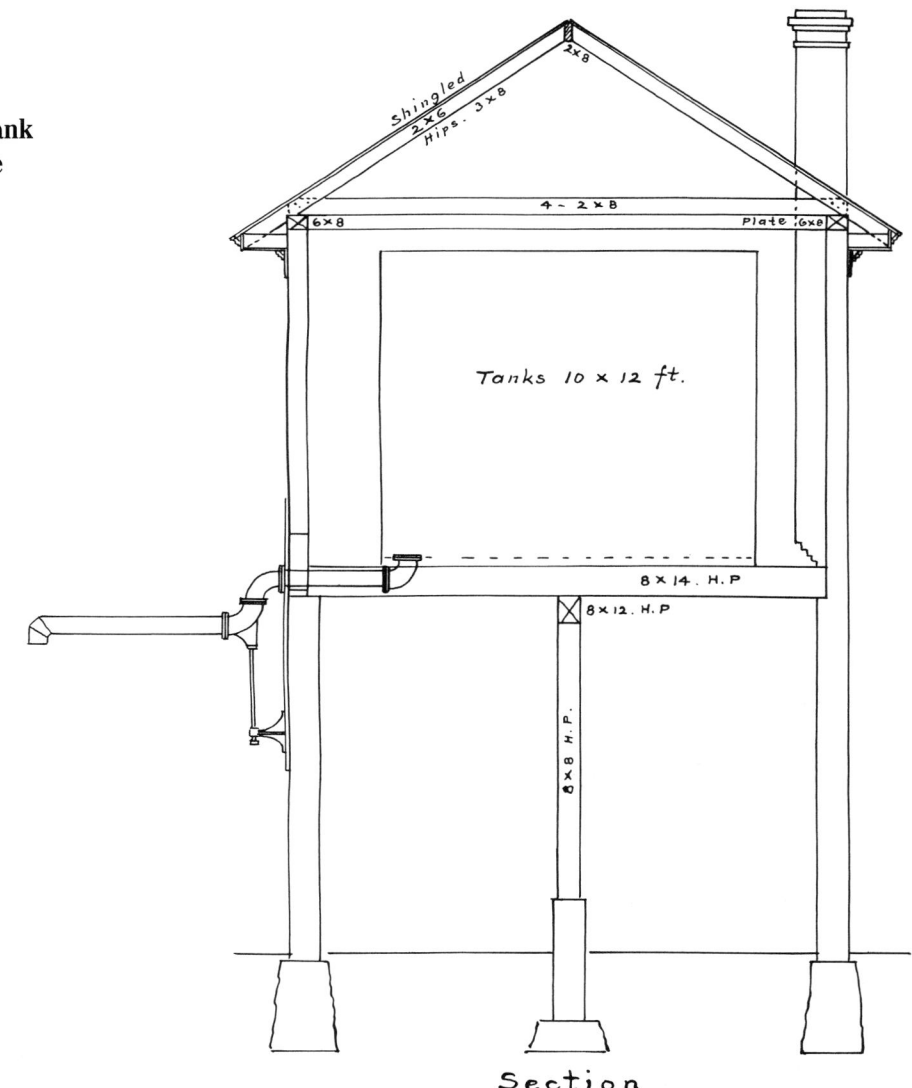

Oakland
West Waterville Station

Old Town
Station, 1904

Poland
Station, 1893, Portland & Rumford Falls Railway
Combination Station by Frederick Danforth, civil engineer, 1894, Portland & Rumford Falls Railway
Poland Corner Station
Empire Combination Station by Frederick Danforth, civil engineer, 1894, Portland & Rumford Falls Railway
Poland Spring Junction Station, 1893
Poland Spring Station, 1893
Poland Spring Station by Frederick Danforth, civil engineer, 1894, Portland & Rumford Falls Railway
Poland Spring Freight House by Frederick Danforth, civil engineer, 1898, Portland & Rumford Falls Railway

Side Elevation drawing for a Blacksmith Shop at Rumford Falls, Portland & Rumford Falls Railway, November, 1894

Portland
Office Building, Commercial Street
Office Building, Portland & Ogdensburg Railway

Randolph
Engine House by E. E. Lewis, architect
Freight Shed by E. E. Lewis, architect, 1890,
Kennebec Central Railroad Station by E. E. Lewis, architect, 1890,
    Kennebec Central Railroad

Rumford
Blacksmith Shop, 1894, Portland & Rumford Falls Railway
Coal Shed, 1896, Portland & Rumford Falls Railway
Engine House (radial) by E. E. Lewis, architect and Frederick
    Danforth, civil engineer, Portland & Rumford Falls Railway
Combination Station by E. E. Lewis, architect and Frederick Danforth,
    civil engineer, 1892, Portland & Rumford Falls Railway

APPENDIX B

Station by E. E. Lewis, architect, 1893, Portland & Rumford Falls Railway
Tool House, Portland & Rumford Falls Railway
Tool House, 1894, Portland & Rumford Falls Railway

Strong
Freight Station, 1890, Sandy River Railroad

The Forks Plantation
Lake Moxie Agent's Residence, Somerset Railway
Mosquito Station, Somerset Railway

Waterville
Building for Office, Baggage and American Express
Station by Gridley J. F. Bryant and Lewis P. Rogers of Boston, architects

Whitefield
Station, 1889

Wilton
Station by Thomas Holt, architect, 1873

Winthrop
Maranacook Station, 1903

Unidentified Location
Tool House, 1894, Portland & Rumford Falls Railway
Freight Office Building, 1900, Sandy River Railroad

MAINE HISTORICAL SOCIETY COLLECTION

Anson
North Anson Station, 1916, Box 5
North Anson Station alterations, 1930, Box 4

Auburn
Coal Shed, 1930, Box 1
Freight House and Office, 1913, Box 4
Danville Junction Station, 1901, Box 5
Danville Junction Station, 1909, Box 4

Augusta
Baggage Rooms, 1905, Box 4
Freight House, 1912, Box 4
Riverside Station, Box 4

Bangor
Coal Storage Run, Box 1
Sand House, 1945, Box 1

Bath
Engine House and Boiler Room, 1889, Box 3

Belgrade
Station, 1905, Box 5
North Belgrade Freight House, 1914, Box 5

Bingham
Engine House, 1924, Box 3

Bowdoinham
Freight and Baggage Room, 1892, Box 4

Bridgton
Station, Box 6
Station Alterations, 1919, Box 6

Brooks
Station, 1892, Box 4

Brunswick
Coaling Plant, 1914, Box 1
Engine House Addition, 1904, Box 3
Store House, Box 1
Yard Office Building, 1907, Box 4

Byron
Houghton Turntable, 1899, Rumford Falls & Rangeley Lakes
   Railroad, Box 3

Canton
Gilbertville Station by E. E. Lewis, architect and Frederick Danforth,
   civil engineer, January, 1892, Box 4
Meadowview Station, 1902, Portland & Rumford Falls Railway,
   Box 5
Station, 1904, Portland & Rumford Falls Railway, Box 5

Carmel
Station, 1908, Box 4

Clinton
Station Alterations, 1949, Box 5

Cornish
Freight House Alterations, 1907, Box 5

APPENDIX B

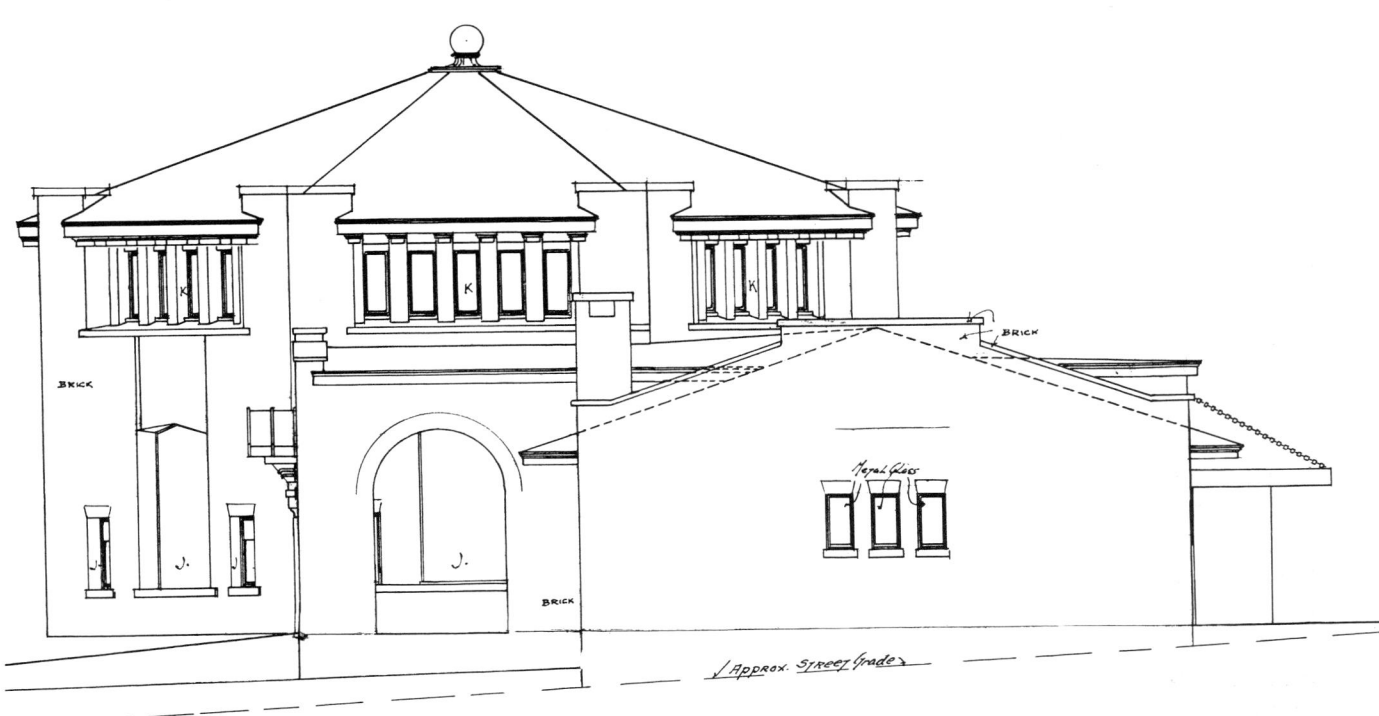

North Elevation drawing by Robert C. Reamer for a Passenger Station at Augusta, Maine Central Railroad, n.d.

Corinna
Spragues Mill Station and Freight House, 1902, Box 4

Cumberland
Station, Box 5

Danforth
Water Tower, 1897, Box 1

Davis Township
Johns Brook Engineers Camp, Rangeley Lakes & Megantic, Box 5

Dexter
Baggage and Express Building Alterations, 1922, Box 3
Silvers Mills Station and Freight House, 1891, Box 4

Dixfield
Freight House by Frederick Danforth, civil engineer, Box 4
Freight House by E. E. Lewis, architect, 1892, Portland & Rumford Falls Railway, Box 7
Station by E. E. Lewis, architect and Frederick Danforth, civil engineer, November, 1893, Box 4
Station Alterations, 1905, Box 4

Eastport
Pengoyd Standard Turntable, 1898, Box 7

ALONG THE RAILS

End elevation drawing for Depots at Greene, Leeds, Monmouth, Belgrade [Androscoggin & Kennebec Railroad], 1849

Enfield
Station, Box 4

Fairfield
Freight House, Box 5
Tower, Box 1

Falmouth
West Falmouth Station, Box 5

Farmington
Engine House, 1909, Box 3

Farmington
West Farmington Station, 1904, Box 4

Gardiner
South Gardiner Freight House Alterations, 1924, Box 4

Gorham
White Rock Station Alterations, 1916, Box 5

Gray
Freight House and Tank, 1914, Box 4
Freight House, 1914, Box 5

Hancock
Engine House, Box 3
Station and Freight House, 1902, Box 5
Washington Junction Engine House, 1923, Box 3

Harmony
Engine and Tank House, 1912, Box 3
Freight House, 1912, Box 4
Station, 1912, Box 4

Hartland
Station Addition, 1918, Box 4

Hermon
Hermon Center Station, 1908, Box 4
Hermon Pond Station, 1909, Box 4
Northern Maine Junction Station Alterations, 1914, Box 5

Hiram
Bridgton Junction Coal Shed, 1920, Box 6

Jay
Chisholms Mills Station, Box 5, "to be taken down and re-erected at Cathance [Topsham], 1911"
North Jay Station, 1894, Box 4
Otis Falls Station, 1896, Box 5

Leeds
Leeds Center Station Alterations, 1907, Box 4
Leeds Center Station and Freight House, 1908, Box 5

Lewiston
Engine House Foundation, 1919, Box 3
Engine House, 1926, Box 3
Engine House, 1943, Box 3
500 Ton Coaling Station, 1923, Box 1
500 Ton Coal Station, Box 3
Freight House, 1900, Box 5
Lower Station Alterations, 1886, Box 4

Lincoln
Freight House and Platform, 1951, Box 4

Livermore
Freight House, Portland & Rumford Falls Railway, Box 4

Livermore Falls
Freight House, 1898, Box 4

Madrid
Reeds Mill Station and Freight Shed, Phillips & Rangeley Railroad, Box 6

Mattawamkeag
Baggage Room, 1910, Box 5

Monmouth
Annabessacook Station, 1918, Box 4

Moscow
Deadwater Station with Residence, 1913, Box 4

Newcastle
Damariscotta Mills Station, 1903, Box 4

Newport
Baggage and Express Room Alterations, 1903, Box 4
Newport Junction Water Tank, Chicago Bridge Iron Works, 1925, Box 3

Nobleboro
Station, Box 4

Norridgewock
Station Alterations, Box 5

Oakland
Office Building, 1909, Box 4
Station, 1909, Box 4
Station, 1941, Box 5

Old Town
50,000 Gallon Tank, 1925, Box 5
Freight House Alterations, Box 5
Water Tank, Chicago Bridge & Iron Works, 1925, Box 3
Great Works Station, 1890, Box 4

Oquossoc
Engine House, Rumford Falls & Rangeley Lakes Railroad, Box 3
Station Alterations, 1922, Box 1

Passadumkeag
Station, Box 4

Phillips
Engine House, 1923, Box 6

APPENDIX B

ELEVATION.

Elevation drawing for a Passenger Station at Maranacook [Maine Central Railroad], May, 1903

Poland
Freight House by Frederick Danforth, civil engineer, Box 4
Station, Box 4
Station Alterations, 1929, Box 4

Portland
American Express Building, Box 4
American Express Building Additions, Union Station, Box 4
American Express Building, 1920, Box 5
Car Repair Shop, Thompson's Point, 1903, Box 3
Engine House No. 3, 1915, Box 1
Fore River Signal Tower, 1923, Portland Terminal Co., Box 1
Garage and Sawdust Bin, 1935, REA, Box 3
Heating Plant, 1916, Box 3
Paint Shop, Thompson's Point, 1895, Box 3
Shed for American Express Company, 1906, Box 4
Union Station Site Plan by W. Bleddyn Powell, architect, January 22, 1887, Box 5
Union Station by Bradlee, Winslow & Wetherell of Boston, 1888, Principal Elevation, Box 4
Union Station Addition, 1907, Box 4
Brighton Junction Coal Shed, 1912, Box 6
Deering Junction Sand House, 1910, Boston & Maine, Box 3

Rangeley
Bemis Engine House, Rumford Falls & Rangeley Lakes Railroad, Box 3
Bemis Engine House (radial), Rumford Falls & Rangeley Lakes Railroad, Box 3
South Rangeley Station, Rumford Falls & Rangeley Lakes Railroad, Box 4

Elevation drawing for a Baggage Room for Glen Station and Fryeburg [Maine Central Railroad], no date

Readfield
Baggage Room, 1903, Box 5
Freight Building, 1905, Box 4

Richmond
Iceboro Station, Box 5

Rockland
Engine House Additions and Alterations, September, 1920, Box 3
Engine House, March, 1921, Box 3
Monitor Engine House, September, 1919, Box 3

Rockwood Strip
Kineo Three Stall Engine House, 1914, Box 3

Rumford
Engine House by E. E. Lewis, architect and Frederick Danforth, civil engineer, 1892, Box 4
Section House, 1914, Box 1
Station by E. E. Lewis, architect, April, 1893, Box 4
Station Alterations, 1941, Box 4

Solon
Station Alterations, 1911, Box 7

APPENDIX B

South Portland
Coal and Sand Station, 1923, Portland Terminal Co., Box 1
Engine House Additions, Rigby, Box 3
Ice House, 1922, Portland Terminal Co., Box 1
Mellin Universal Conveyor, 1923, Box 1
Miscellaneous Structures, 1923, Portland Terminal Co., Box 1
Motor Car Section House, 1923, Box 1
Sand Bins, 1954, Box 1
Sand Tower, 1923, Box 3
Skunk Hill Signal Tower, 1923, Portland Terminal Co., Box 1

Standish
Sebago Lake Engine House, 1888, Box 3

Stetsontown Township
Kennebago Engine House and Tank House, 1912, Rangeley Lakes & Megantic, Box 3

Thorndike
Station, Box 4

Elevation — Track Front — drawing for a Gateman's House [Maine Central Railroad], Portland, c. 1890

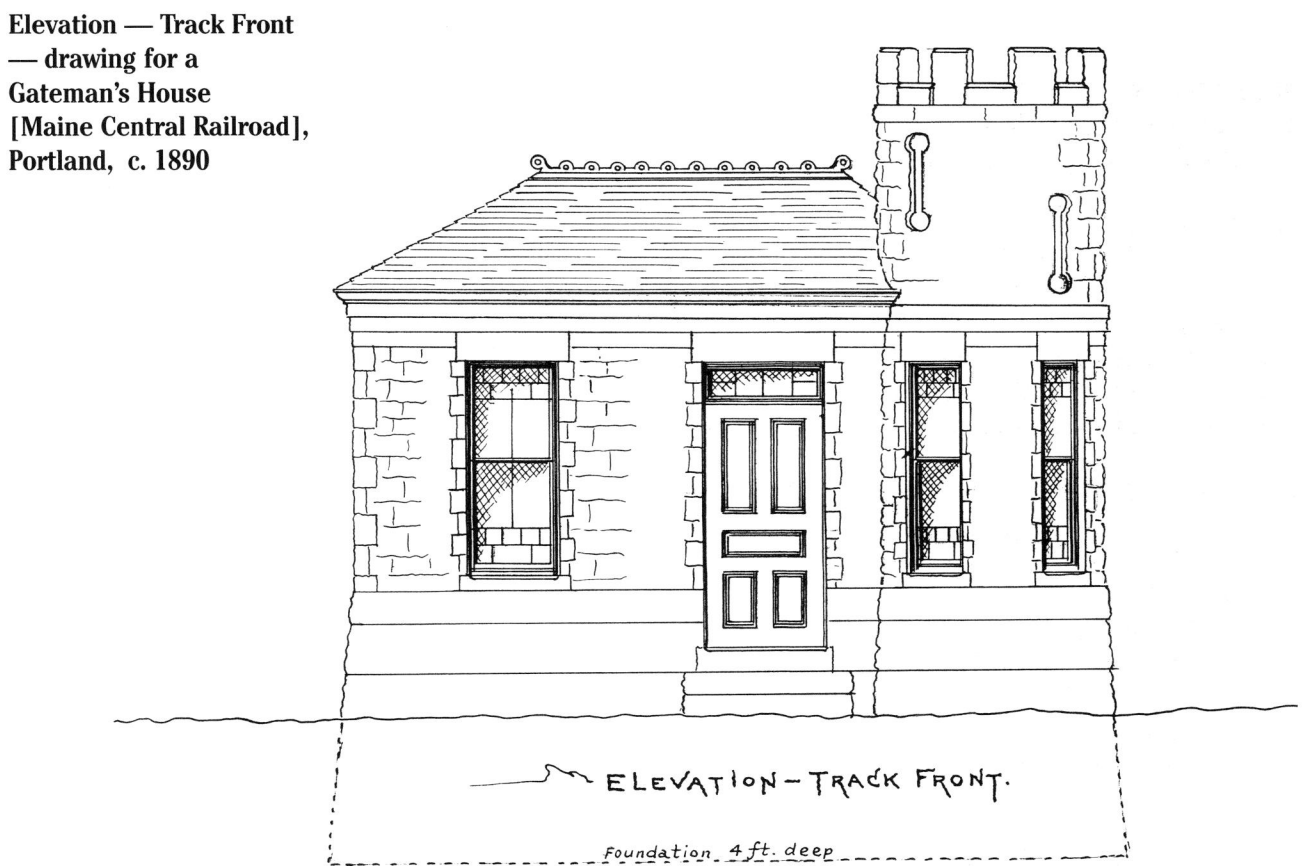

Vanceboro
Cow Sheds, 1946, Box 1
Employee Rooms in Old Tank House, 1898, Box 1
Engine House, 1882, Box 3
Freight House, 1915, Box 5
Six Stall Engine House, 1912, Box 3
Pengoyd Standard Turntable, 1898, Box 7
Station Addition, 1917, Box 4
Station Alterations, Box 5
Water Tank, Box 1

Veazie
Station, 1907, Box 4

Waterville
Coal Derrick, 1897, Box 1
Coaling Station, 1915, Box 1

Windham
South Windham Station, Box 4

Winthrop
Maranacook Pavilion, Box 5

Woolwich
Station and Freight House, 1903, Box 4
Station, 1927, Box 4